KANJI PAGE LOCATOR

開 14	味 15	新 16	集 17	有 18	以 19	医 20	意 21
急 22	院 23	員 24	動 25	映 26	写 27	英 28	駅 29
終 30	起 31	送 32	教 33	主 34	重 35	親 36	界 37
貸 38	通 39	体 40	借 41	代 42	漢 43	館 44	究 45
業 46	着 47	銀 48	研 49	験 50	試 51	事 52	転 53
去 54	質 55	品 56	死 57	図 58	住 59	族 60	注 61
題 62	建 63	旅 64	使 65	仕 66	度 67	問 68	堂 69
特 70	習 71	飲 72	場 73	計 74	運 75	始 76	発 77
不 78	服 79	真 80	待 81	自 82	飯 83	用 84	持 85
者 86	物 87	屋 88	安 89	病 90	世 91	曜 92	私 93

MANGA UNIVERSITY presents...

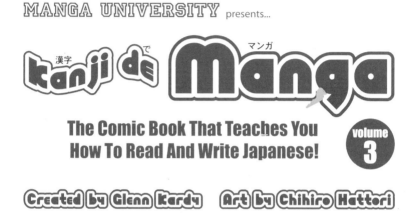

漢字 で マンガ
kanji de Manga

The Comic Book That Teaches You How To Read And Write Japanese!

volume **3**

Created by Glenn Kardy   Art by Chihiro Hattori

Japanime

TOKYO   SAN FRANCISCO

Manga Univer   presents ... Kanji de Manga
The Comic Book That Teaches You
How To Read And Write Japanese!
Volume Three

ISBN 4-921205-04-3

Published by Japanime Co. Ltd.
Japanime Bldg. 2F
3-31-18 Nishi-Kawaguchi
Kawaguchi-shi, Saitama 332-0021
Japan

First edition
Printed in Japan in September 2005

This book belongs to:

名前 _____

THE MANGA UNIVERSITY
MISSION STATEMENT

THE MISSION OF MANGA UNIVERSITY IS TO ENLIGHTEN AND EDUCATE THE INTERNATIONAL COMMUNITY ON ALL ASPECTS OF JAPANESE CULTURE THROUGH THE CREATIVE USE OF TRADITIONAL MANGA ARTWORK.

THE UNIVERSITY RECOGNIZES THAT MANGA TRANSCENDS MAINSTREAM ENTERTAINMENT AND POSSESSES A UNIQUE ABILITY TO CONVEY THE TRUE SPIRIT OF JAPAN, MAKING THE ART FORM AN IDEAL COMMUNICATIVE TOOL TO TOUCH THE LIVES AND INSPIRE THE MINDS OF JAPAN ENTHUSIASTS WORLDWIDE.

OUR MISSION AND PHILOSOPHY ARE FIRMLY ROOTED IN THE PRINCIPLES AND CONVICTION OF THE JAPANESE EDUCATIONAL TRADITION AND IN THE BEST IDEALS OF JAPANESE HERITAGE.

FOUNDED AT THE TURN OF THE CENTURY AND LOCATED IN TOKYO, MANGA UNIVERSITY IS ONE OF THE WORLD'S FOREMOST PUBLISHERS OF MANGA-THEMED EDUCATIONAL MATERIALS.

CONTENTS

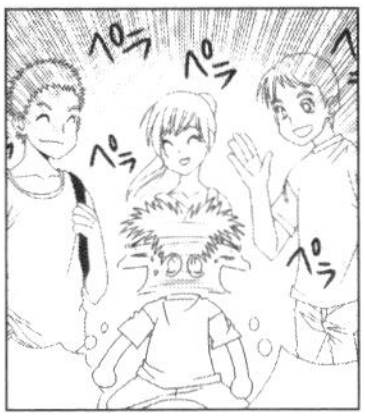
ペラ
ペラ
ペラ
ペラ

INTRODUCTION

Congratulations! The faculty of Manga University is proud to have dedicated students like you. And if you've already completed the first two volumes in the *Kanji de Manga* series, you probably have noticed for yourself how your hard work has paid off.

How many times now have you seen some Japanese writing and been able to recognize the characters? Let's face it: You are in elite company! Outside of the Japanese themselves, very few people can read and write as well as you do at this point.

Yes, there is still a lot to learn. But undoubtedly, what started off as a journey into an unknown world filled with strange characters is starting to feel like a trip through fun and familiar territory.

Right now, you know 160 kanji (if you've finished studying the first two volumes). That may not sound like a lot when you consider the seemingly endless number of characters in existence. But when you think about how you've lived so much of your life with a mere 26 letters of the alphabet,160 kanji is an impressive amount!

And soon, you'll learn even more. This book will teach you another 80 kanji, all of which are needed to pass the third level of the Japanese Language Proficiency Test. (For more information about the test, please see page 94.) In Japan, these characters are taught between the second and fifth grades of grammar school. With just a few more months of study and memorization, you'll be able to read Japanese newspaper headlines, your favorite manga stories, and Japanese Web sites – some of which you can probably already decipher with the 160 characters you have already learned.

Take a moment and flip through the pages of this book. All of the characters here are new, but certainly they don't look as alien and terrifying as they did when you saw your very first kanji. In fact, instead of being a little unsure of yourself, you are probably confident that soon, all of these characters will be mainstays in your increasingly impressive syllabary.

If not, don't worry. We're going to make it as easy as possible, and all your favorite manga friends are here to help.

And now we're going to let you in on a little secret: Not everyone makes it this far. You are among the best of the best. And experience tells us that if you've made it this far, you are among the select few who are likely to go all the way.

That's right – by continuing your lessons, you are rapidly moving toward the ultimate goal of all serious linguistic students: total mastery of a language, including complete written fluency.

That may sound like some distant goal, but it's really not that far away. And the fact that you are taking steps on your own means that you are among the most dedicated students in the world.

That's why we at Manga University are so proud – not only of all you have accomplished so far, but proud that you continue to educate yourself with us.

To show how proud of you we here at Manga University are, we have a gift for you when you've completed the lessons in this book. At a special Web site only for Manga University students, your very first degree in Kanji Arts is waiting. All you need to do is print it and frame it – and continue to learn to earn higher degrees. You can download your diploma here:

http://www.mangauniversity.com/diploma/kjdm3.html

PAGE GUIDE

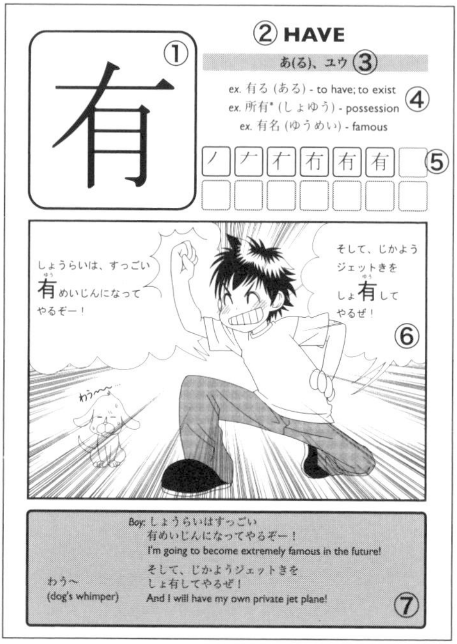
① 有
② HAVE
あ(る)、ユウ ③
ex. 有る (ある) - to have; to exist
ex. 所有* (しょゆう) - possession
ex. 有名 (ゆうめい) - famous
④
⑤
しょうらいは、すっごい 有めいじんになって やるぞー！
そして、じかよう ジェットきを しょ有して やるぜ！
⑥
Boy: しょうらいはすっごい
有めいじんになってやるぞー！
I'm going to become extremely famous in the future!
そして、じかようジェットきを
しょ有してやるぜ！
And I will have my own private jet plane!
わう〜
(dog's whimper)
⑦

① The featured kanji

② Common definition

③ Readings: kun-yomi (Japanese readings) are written in hiragana, while on-yomi (Chinese readings) are in katakana.

④ Examples of compounds containing the featured kanji, their pronunciations (in hiragana) and English definitions. (An asterisk next to a compound indicates that one or more of its kanji are not featured in this or any of the previous volumes of the "Kanji de Manga" series.)

⑤ Stroke order: In general, the strokes are written from top to bottom and left to right. For a list of additional stroke-order rules, please refer to the chart at the back of this book.

⑥ The manga. All dialogue is written in hiragana and katakana except for the single featured kanji. The proper pronunciation of the kanji is indicated in furigana (tiny hiragana) written above the character.

⑦ Translation of the dialogue and selected onomatopoeia.

Kanji de Manga

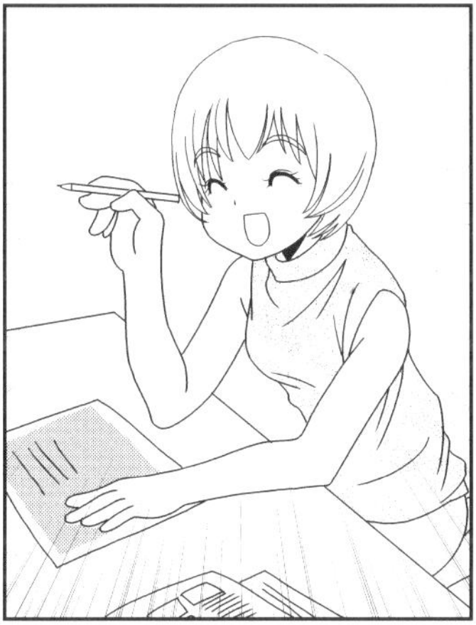

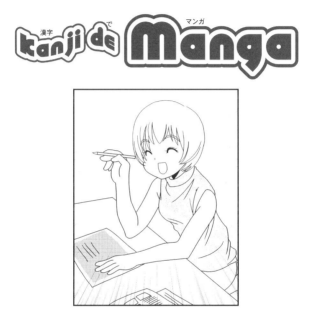

STUDY SECTION

開

OPEN

あ(く)、あ(ける)、ひら(く)、カイ

ex. 開く (あく、ひらく) - to open
ex. 開会式* (かいかいしき) - opening ceremony
ex. 開店 (かいてん) - grand opening (of a store)

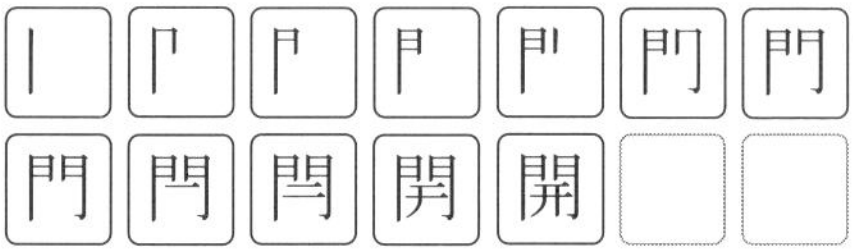

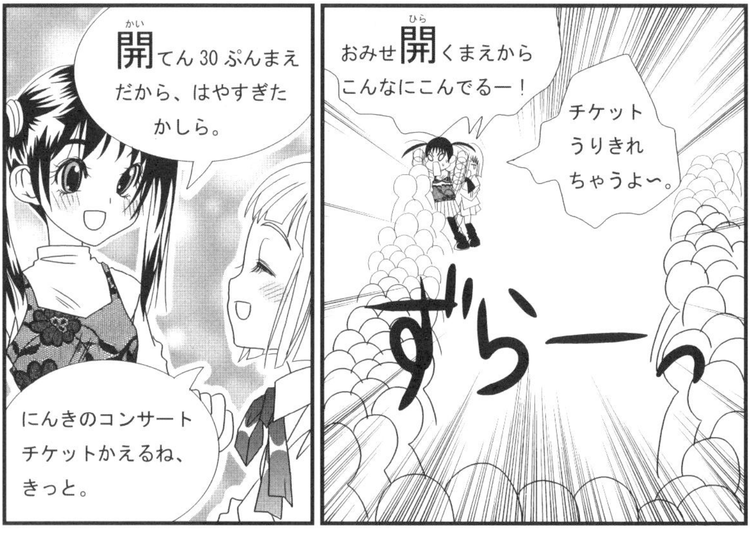
開てん 30 ぷんまえだから、はやすぎたかしら。
にんきのコンサートチケットかえるね、きっと。
おみせ開くまえからこんなにこんでるー！
チケットうりきれちゃうよ〜。
ずらーっ

First girl: 開てん30ぷんまえだから、はやすぎたかしら。
We may be too early; it's still 30 minutes before the shop opens.

Second girl: にんきのコンサートチケットかえるね、きっと。
We shouldn't have any trouble buying tickets to the concert.

First girl: おみせ開くまえからこんなにこんでるー！
The shop hasn't opened yet and it's already packed!

Second girl: チケットうりきれちゃうよ〜。
The tickets may already be sold out.

ずらーっ (long line of people)

TASTE

あじ、あじ(わう)、ミ

ex. 塩味* (しおあじ) - salty
ex. 興味* (きょうみ) - interest
ex. 味覚* (みかく) - taste

味

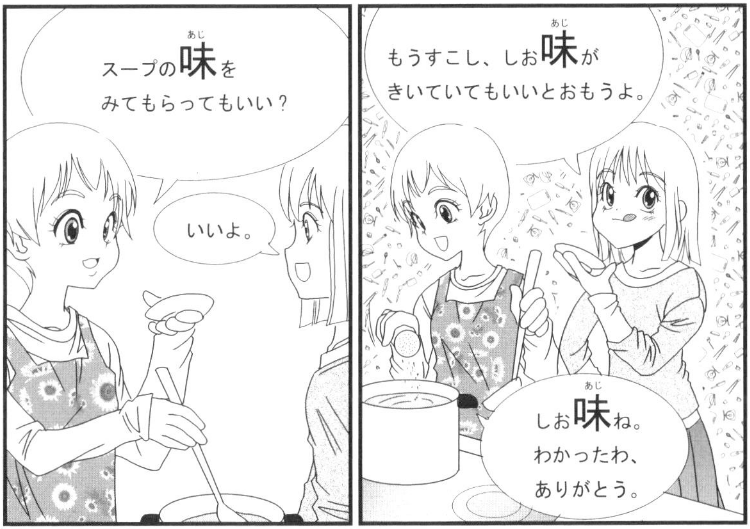
スープの味(あじ)を
みてもらってもいい？
いいよ。
もうすこし、しお味(あじ)が
きいていてもいいとおもうよ。
しお味(あじ)ね。
わかったわ、
ありがとう。

Girl on left: スープの味を
みてもらってもいい？
Could you taste my soup?

Girl on right: いいよ。
Sure.

Girl on right: もうすこし、しお味が
きいていてもいいとおもうよ。
I think it needs a bit more salt.

Girl on left: しお味ね。わかったわ、
ありがとう。
More salt. OK, thanks.

新

NEW

あたら(しい)、あら(た)、シン

ex. 新しい (あたらしい) - new
ex. 新年 (しんねん) - new year
ex. 新品 (しんぴん) - brand-new item

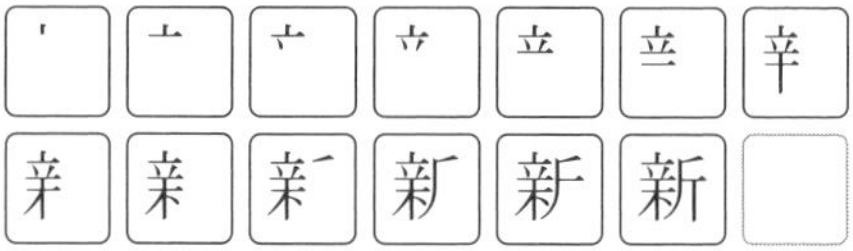

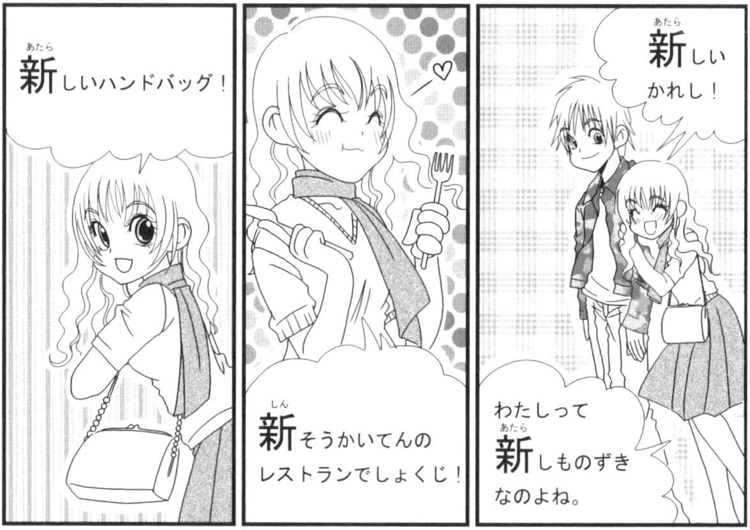
新しいハンドバッグ！
新そうかいてんの
レストランでしょくじ！
新しい
かれし！
わたしって
新しものずき
なのよね。

Girl: 新しいハンドバッグ！
A new handbag!

新そうかいてんの
レストランでしょくじ！
Dinner at a new restaurant!

新しいかれし！
My new boyfriend!

わたしって新しものずき
なのよね。
I love things that are brand-new!

COLLECT

あつ(まる)、あつ(める)、シュウ

ex. 集める (あつめる) - to collect
ex. 集会 (しゅうかい) - assembly
ex. 収集* (しゅうしゅう) - collection

| ノ | イ | イ´ | イ⺅ | 什 | 伴 | 隹 |
| 隹 | 隼 | 隼 | 集 | 集 | | |

Girl: すごーい！
こんなにきって集めたの？
Awesome! You've collected
all these stamps?

Boy: うん。
Yup.

Boy: きってしゅう集は、ちいさい
ころからのしゅみだからね。
けっこう集まったよ。
I've been collecting stamps since I was
a little boy. I've got quite a few now.

Girl: そうだったんだ。
I see.

HAVE

あ(る)、ユウ

ex. 有る (ある) - to have; to exist
ex. 所有* (しょゆう) - possession
ex. 有名 (ゆうめい) - famous

| ノ | ナ | 才 | 右 | 有 | 有 | |

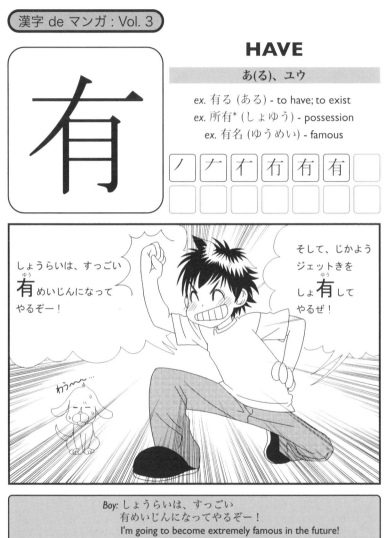

Boy: しょうらいは、すっごい 有めいじんになってやるぞー!	I'm going to become extremely famous in the future!
わう〜 (dog's whimper)	そして、じかようジェットきを しょ有してやるぜ! And I will have my own private jet plane!

BY ALL MEANS

イ

ex. 以外 (いがい) - except
ex. 以後 (いご) - since; after; in the future
ex. 以上 (いじょう) - more than; that's all

| 丨 | レ | 𧘇 | 以 | 以 | | |

これ以_いがいで
かっていない
ものは…と。

あぁ、
あった
これね。

これ以_いじょう
かいものするの
やめようよー！

はやくー。

もう、
もちきれ
ないよ〜。

ふら…

ふら…

ふら…

Girl (reading shopping list): これ以がいで
　かっていないものは…と。
　The things I haven't bought
　except for these are...

あぁ、あったこれね。
Oh, yes. Here they are.

Boyfriend: これ以じょうかいものするの
　やめようよー！
　We should stop shopping already!
　もう、もちきれないよ〜。
　I can't carry anymore.

Girl: はやくー。 Hurry.

ふらふら… (staggering)

医

MEDICINE / DOCTOR

イ

ex. 医者 (いしゃ) - doctor
ex. 医療* (いりょう) - medical treatment
ex. 獣医* (じゅうい) - veterinarian

はーい。
ちゅうしゃをしますからねー。
いやだー！やめてくれー！
こわいよー！わー！わぁぁぁぁぁ！
医しゃがちゅうしゃをいやがってどうするんですか?!
医しゃが！
医しゃだっていやなものはいやなんだー！

Nurse: はーい。
OK.
ちゅうしゃをしますからねー。
Here comes your shot.

Doctor: いやだー！やめてくれー！
Noooo! Stop!
こわいよー！わー！わぁぁぁぁぁ！
I'm scared! Ugh! Ahhhhhh!

Nurse: 医しゃがちゅうしゃをいやがってどうするんですか?! 医しゃが！
Doctors are not supposed to be afraid of needles! You are a doctor!

Doctor: 医しゃだっていやなものはいやなんだー！
Even doctors are afraid of things that are frightening!

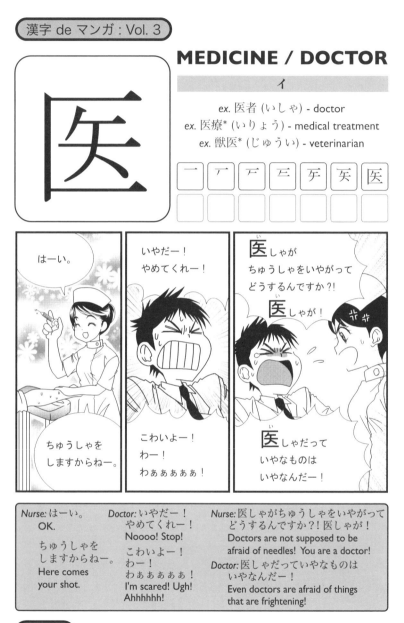

MIND / MEANING

イ

ex. 意見 (いけん) - opinion
ex. 意味 (いみ) - meaning
ex. 注意* (ちゅうい) - attention

むにょーん (sound of stretching face)	*Big brother:* よろしく。 Please?	*Neighbor:* 意みが わかんないよー！ なんで わかるんだー！
ぶにー (sound of blowing air through pursed lips)	*Little brother:* りょうかい。 OK. *Neighbor:* えー！？ いまので意みが つうじたの！？ Huh? Do they understand what each other means just by doing that!?	I just don't get it! How do they do that?! じたばた (sound of shaking with anger)

急

HURRY / SUDDEN

いそ(ぐ)、キュウ

ex. 急ぐ (いそぐ) - hurry
ex. 急行 (きゅうこう) - express train
ex. 至急* (しきゅう) - urgent

ノ	⺈	㔾	刍	刍	刍	急
急	急					

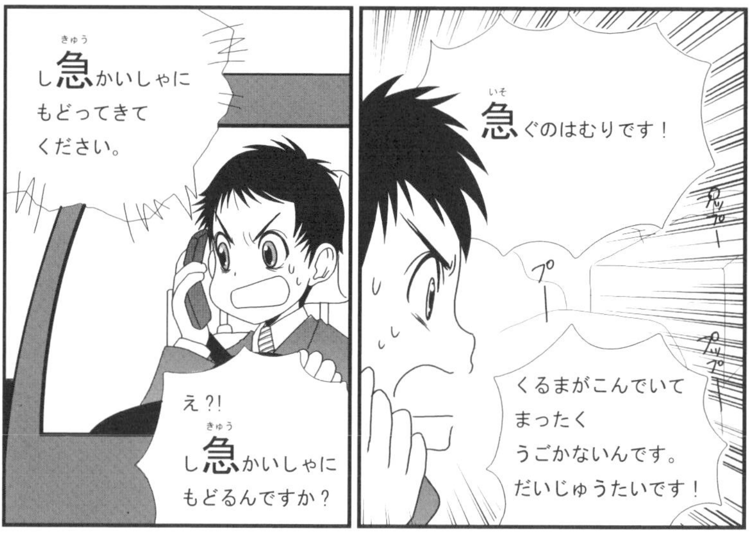

し急かいしゃにもどってきてください。
え?!
し急かいしゃにもどるんですか?
急ぐのはむりです!
プー
プップー
プップー
くるまがこんでいてまったくうごかないんです。だいじゅうたいです!

Voice on telephone: し急かいしゃにもどってきてください。
We urgently need you to return to the office.

Businessman: え?!
し急かいしゃにもどるんですか?
What?! I need to go back to the office right away?

Businessman: 急ぐのはむりです!
It's impossible for me to rush back!
くるまがこんでいてまったくうごかないんです。
There are cars everywhere and I can't move at all.
だいじゅうたいです!
It's a heavy traffic jam!

プー
プップー
(honk honk)

INSTITUTION

院

イン

ex. 病院 (びょういん) - hospital
ex. 大学院 (だいがくいん) - graduate school
ex. 修道院* (しゅうどういん) - monastery

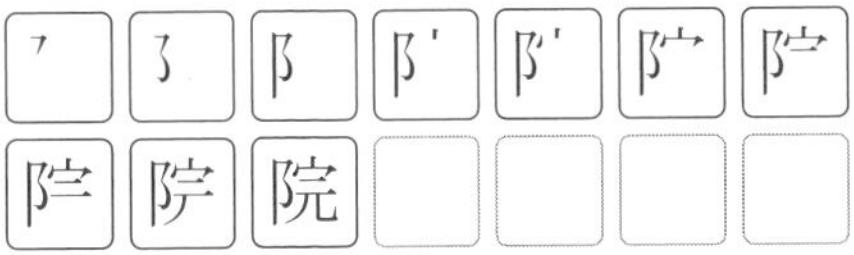

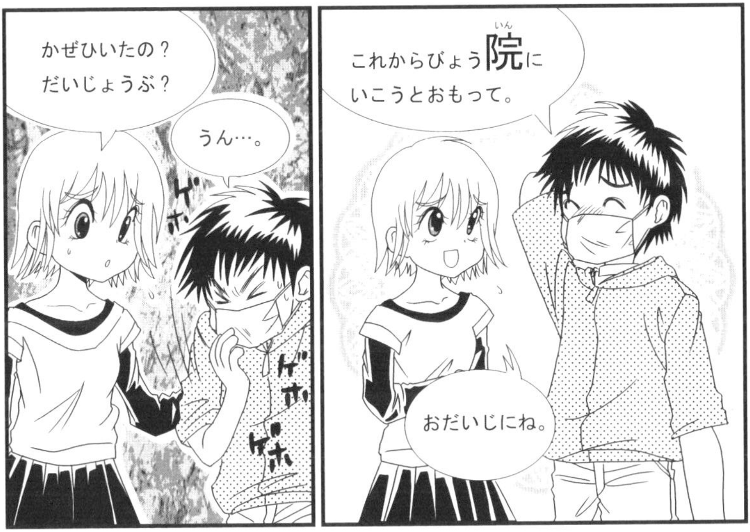
かぜひいたの？
だいじょうぶ？
うん…。
ゲホ
ゲホ
ゲホ
これからびょう院にいこうとおもって。
おだいじにね。

Girl: かぜひいたの？
だいじょうぶ？
You've got a cold?
Are you OK?

Boy: うん…。 Yeah.

ゲホゲホ (coughing)

Boy: これからびょう院にいこうとおもって。
I'm going to the hospital now.

Girl: おだいじにね。
Take care.

(In Japan, people suffering from colds often wear surgical masks to prevent the spread of germs to others.)

員

MEMBER

イン

ex. 委員* (いいん) - committee member
ex. 会員 (かいいん) - club member
ex. 社員 (しゃいん) - company employee

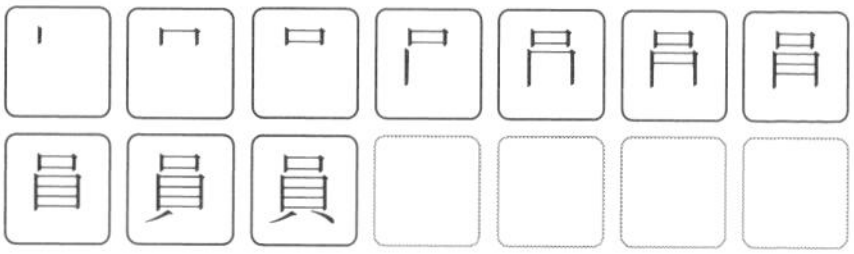

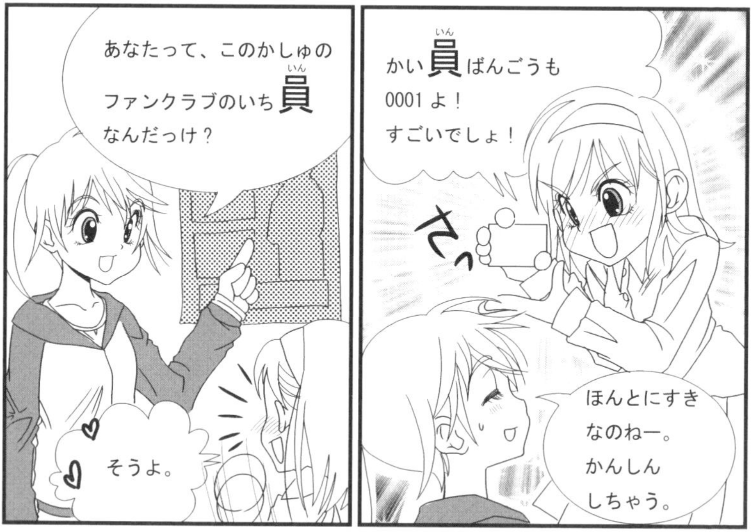
あなたって、このかしゅのファンクラブのいち員(いん)なんだっけ？
そうよ。
かい員(いん)ばんごうも 0001 よ！ すごいでしょ！
さっ
ほんとにすきなのねー。かんしんしちゃう。

Girl on left: あなたって、
このかしゅのファンクラブの
いち員なんだっけ？
Aren't you a member of this singer's fan club?

Girl on right: そうよ。
That's right.

Girl on right: かい員ばんごうも0001よ！
すごいでしょ！
And my membership number is 0001!
Isn't that amazing?

さっ (sound of flashing a card)

Girl on left: ほんとにすきなのねー。
かんしんしちゃう。
You must really like him. I'm impressed.

MOVE

うご(かす)、うご(く)、ドウ

ex. 運動* (うんどう) - exercise
ex. 感動 (かんどう) - impression
ex. 動物 (どうぶつ) - animal

| 一 | 二 | 厂 | 戸 | 台 | 旨 | 重 |
| 重 | 重 | 動 | 動 | | | |

Mother: まいにちうん動する
っていってたけど、きょうは
もうしたの？
You said that you are going to
exercise every day. Are you
already done today?

Boy: え？！ Huh?!

Boy: え…と… えーと…。う… うん…。
あ…いやぁ…。
Um... Well... Y... Yeah... Not really...
しどろしどろ (sound of confusion)

Mother: うわー…。すごく動ようしているわ。
うん動していないのね。
Wow... He seems very flustered. I guess
he isn't really getting enough exercise.

映

REFLECT

うつ(す)、うつ(る)、エイ

ex. 映る (うつる) - to be reflected
ex. 映画館 (えいがかん) - movie theater
ex. 反映* (はんえい) - reflection

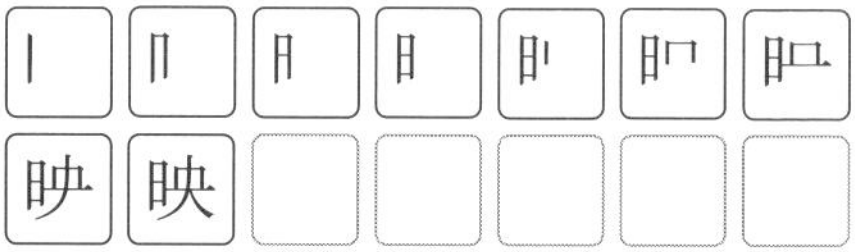

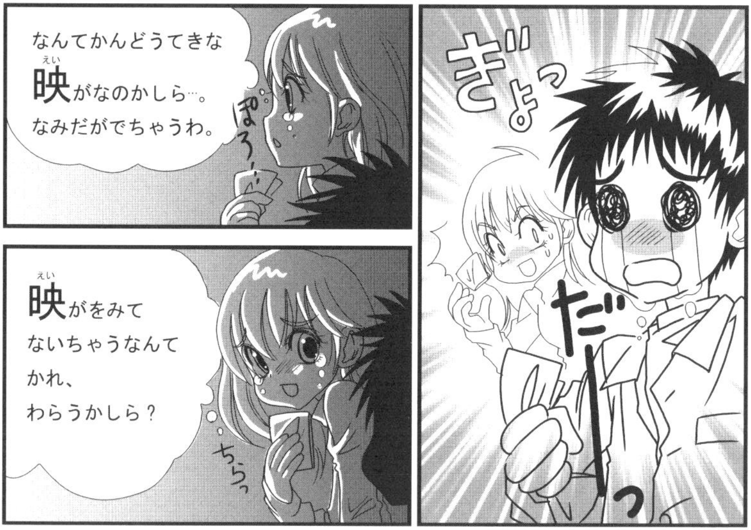
なんてかんどうてきな映(えい)がなのかしら…。なみだがでちゃうわ。
ぽろ…
映(えい)がをみてないちゃうなんてかれ、わらうかしら？
ちらっ
ぎょっ
だーっ

Girl: なんてかんどうてきな映がなのかしら…。なみだがでちゃうわ。
What a touching movie. I can't help but cry.
ぽろ… (sound of single teardrop)
Girl: 映がをみてないちゃうなんてかれ、わらうかしら？
Will he laugh at me for crying at a movie?
ちらっ (glimpse)
ぎょっ
(sound of shock)
だーっ
(an uncontrollable rush of tears)

COPY

うつ(す)、うつ(る)、シャ

ex. 写す (うつす) - to copy; to take a picture
ex. 写生 (しゃせい) - sketch
ex. 写真 (しゃしん) - photograph

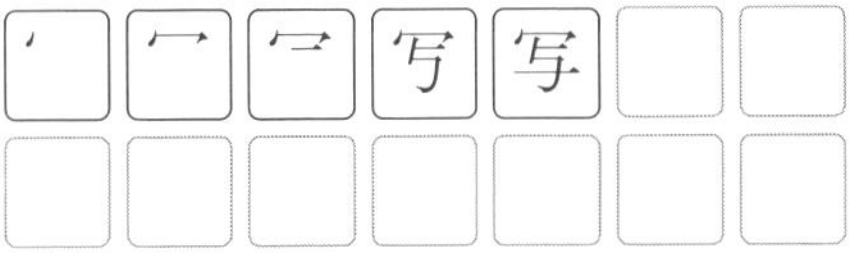

写

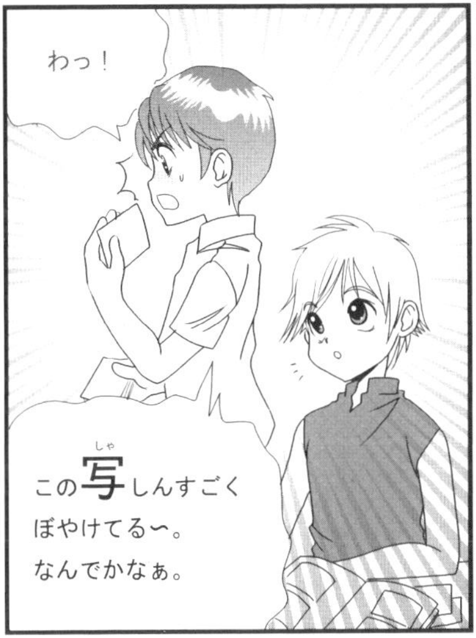
わっ！
この写しんすごくぼやけてる〜。なんでかなぁ。

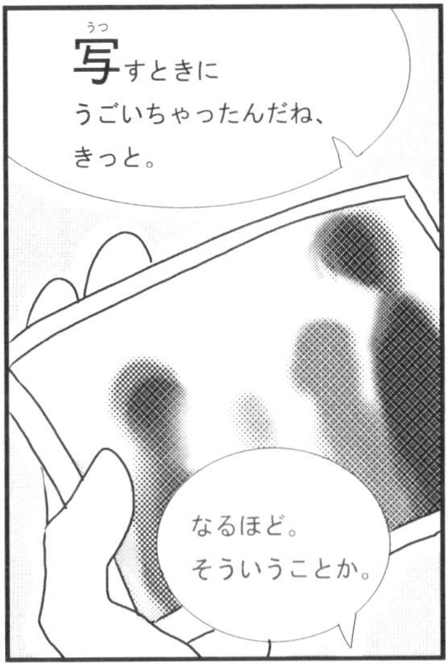
写すときにうごいちゃったんだね、きっと。
なるほど。そういうことか。

Big brother: わっ！
この写しんすごくぼやけてる〜。
なんでかなぁ。
Wow! This photograph is all blurry.
I wonder why.

Little brother: 写すときに
うごいちゃったんだね、きっと。
I suppose you moved the camera
while taking the picture.

Big brother: なるほど。
そういうことか。
Yeah, that's what happened.

英

SUPERB / ENGLISH

エイ

ex. 英会話 (えいかいわ) - English conversation

ex. 英国 (えいこく) - England

ex. 英雄* (えいゆう) - hero

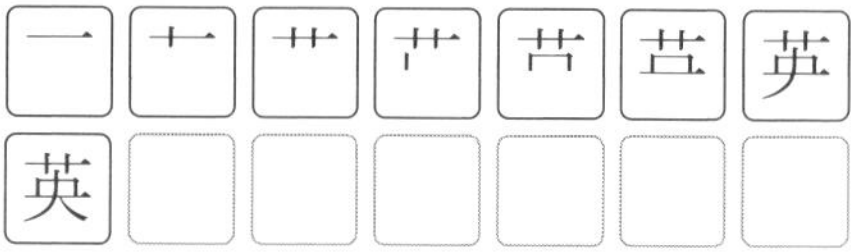

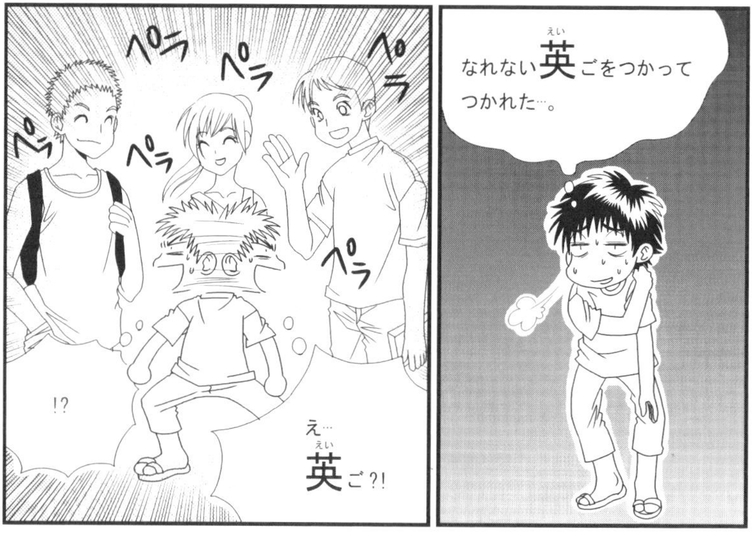
ペラ
ペラ
ペラ
ペラ
ペラ
ペラ
!?
え…
英ご?!
なれない英ごをつかって
つかれた…。

ペラペラ
(Sound of a foreign language being spoken fluently)

Japanese boy: え…　英ご？！
Huh... English?!

Japanese boy: なれない英ごをつかってつかれた…。
Using English makes me exhausted...

STATION

駅

エキ

ex. 駅員 (えきいん) - station employee
ex. 各駅停車*(かくえきていしゃ) - local train
ex. 駅前 (えきまえ) - in front of the station

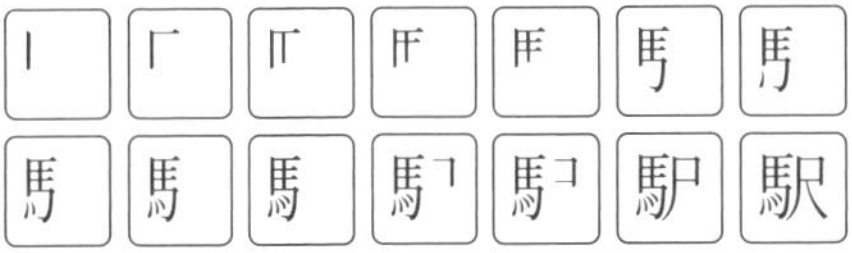

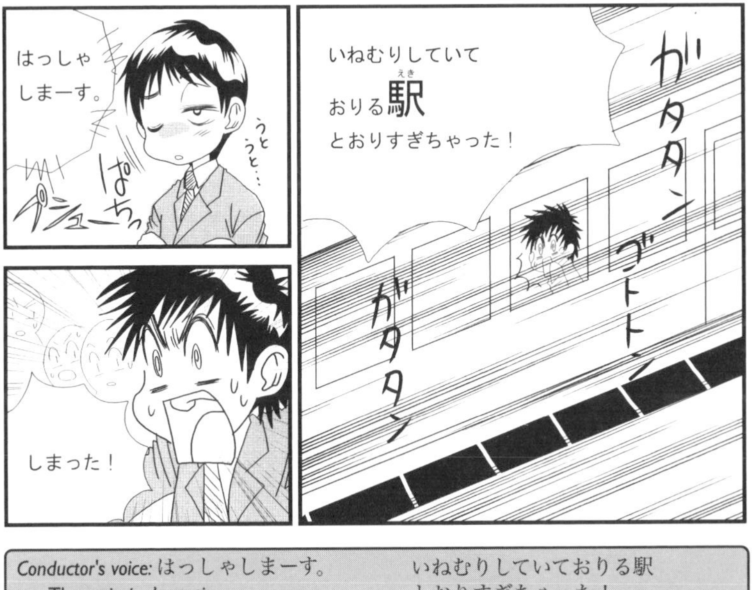
はっしゃ
しまーす。
うとうと…
ぱちっ
プシュー
しまった！
いねむりしていて
おりる駅(えき)
とおりすぎちゃった！
ガタタンゴトトン
ガタタン

Conductor's voice: はっしゃしまーす。
The train is departing.
プシュー (sound of train doors closing)
うとうと… (dozing off)
ぱちっ (opening eyes)
Man: しまった！
Darn!

いねむりしていておりる駅
とおりすぎちゃった！
I fell asleep and passed the station I was supposed to get off at!

ガタタンゴトトン
(sound of train on tracks)

終

END

お(える)、お(わる)、シュウ

ex. 終わる (おわる) - to finish
ex. 終日 (しゅうじつ) - all day long
ex. 終了* (しゅうりょう) - expiration; closing

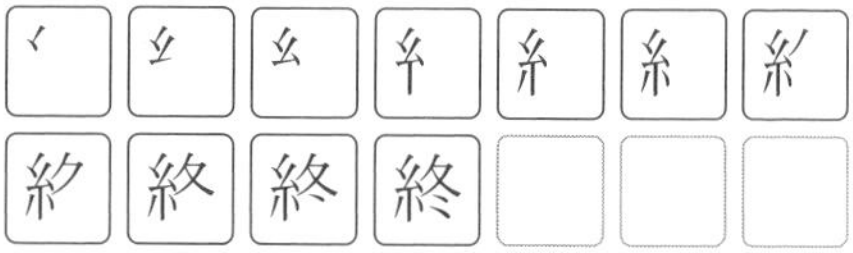

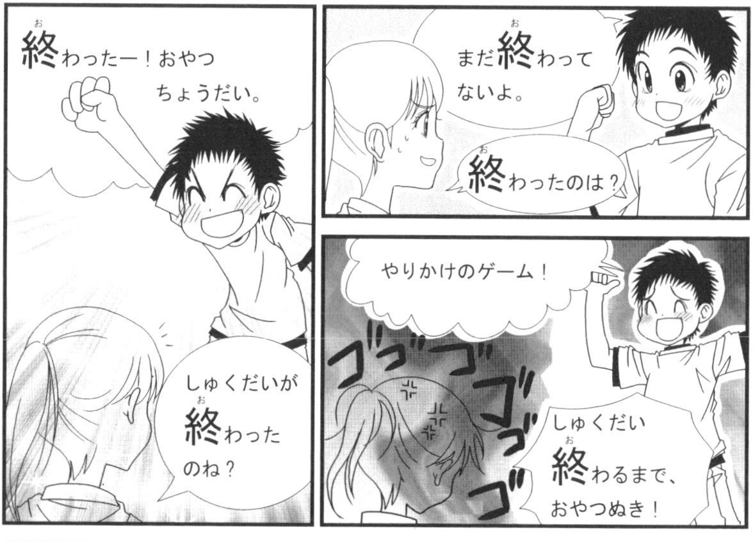
終わったー！おやつちょうだい。
しゅくだいが終わったのね？
まだ終わってないよ。
終わったのは？
やりかけのゲーム！
ゴゴゴゴゴ
しゅくだい終わるまで、おやつぬき！

Boy: 終わったー！ I'm done!
おやつちょうだい。
Can I have my snack now?

Mother: しゅくだいが終わったのね？
You've finished your homework?

Boy: まだ終わってないよ。 No, not yet.

Mother: 終わったのは？ What have you finished?

Boy: やりかけのゲーム！ The computer game!

Mother: しゅくだい終わるまで、おやつぬき！
No snacks until you finish your homework!

ゴゴゴゴゴ (growing anger)

RISE

お(きる)、お(こる)、キ

ex. 起きる (おきる) - to rise; to wake
ex. 縁起物* (えんぎもの) - good luck charm
ex. 起源* (きげん) - origin

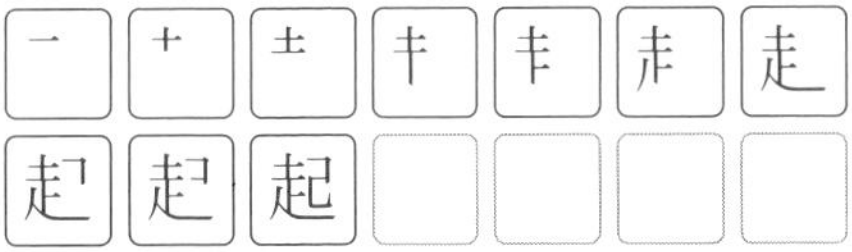

起

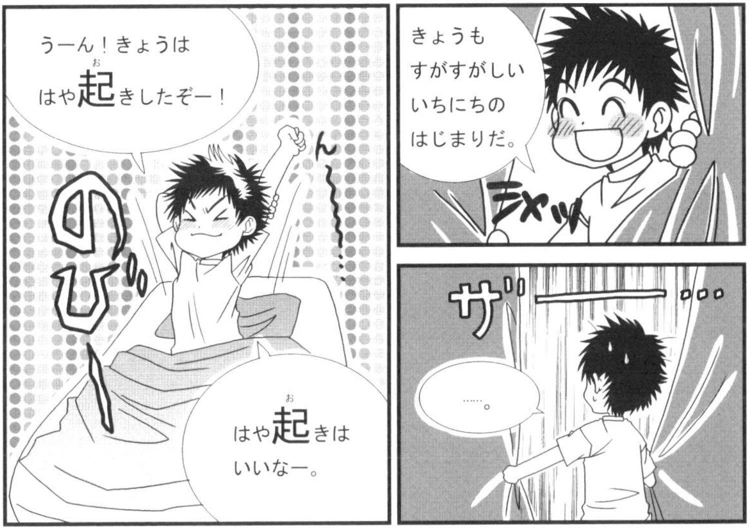

うーん！きょうは はや起(お)きしたぞー！
のびー
ん～～…
はや起(お)きは いいなー。
きょうも すがすがしい いちにちの はじまりだ。
シャッ
ザーー…
……。

Boy: うーん！きょうははや起きしたぞー！
Wow! I woke up early today!
はや起きはいいなー。
It is nice to rise so early.

ん～ Rrrnnn (voiced sound while stretching)

のびー (sound of body stretching)

Boy: きょうもすがすがしい いちにちのはじまりだ。
It's the start of a fresh new day.

シャッ (sound of a curtain being pulled open quickly)

ザー… (sound of heavy rain)

Boy: (speechless)

送

SEND

おく(る)、ソウ

ex. 送る (おくる) - to send
ex. 送料 (そうりょう) - postage
ex. 送別 (そうべつ) - sendoff; farewell

丶	⺍	䒑	兰	关	关	关
关	送					

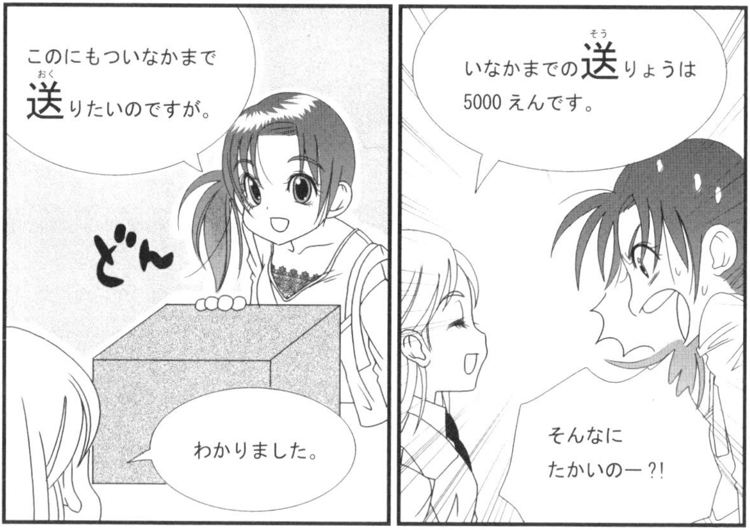
このにもついなかまで
送りたいのですが。
どん
わかりました。
いなかまでの送りょうは
5000 えんです。
そんなに
たかいのー?!

College student: このにもついなかまで送りたいのですが。
I would like to send this parcel to my hometown.

どん (thump)

Postal clerk: わかりました。
I understand.

Postal clerk: いなかまでの送りょうは5000えんです。
The postage to your hometown is 5,000 yen.

College student: そんなにたかいのー？！
Is it that expensive?!

TEACH / RELIGION

おし(える)、おそ(わる)、キョウ

ex. 教師* (きょうし) - teacher
ex. 教会 (きょうかい) - church
ex. 仏教* (ぶっきょう) - Buddhism

| 一 | 十 | 土 | 耂 | 耂 | 孝 | 孝 |
| 孝 | 孝 | 教 | 教 | | | |

きょうもいちにち、いち**教**し
として、

がんばって
べんきょうを
教えるぞー！

がんば
るぞー！
おおっ！！

きょうもせんせい
もえてるね…。

ねっけつ
教し
だよね。

Teacher: きょうもいちにち、
いち教しとして、
がんばってべんきょうを
教えるぞー！
As usual, I'm going to do my best
to serve my students as their
teacher!

Teacher: がんばるぞー！おおっ！
I'm going to work hard! Yes!

Student on right: きょうもせんせい
もえてるね・・・。
As usual, he's all fired up today.

Student on left: ねっけつ教しだよね。
He's a very passionate teacher.

主

MAIN / MASTER

おも、ぬし、シュ

ex. 主 (ぬし) - master
ex. 主な (おもな) - main; chief
ex. 主人公* (しゅじんこう) - hero; heroine

丶	亠	亍	丰	主		

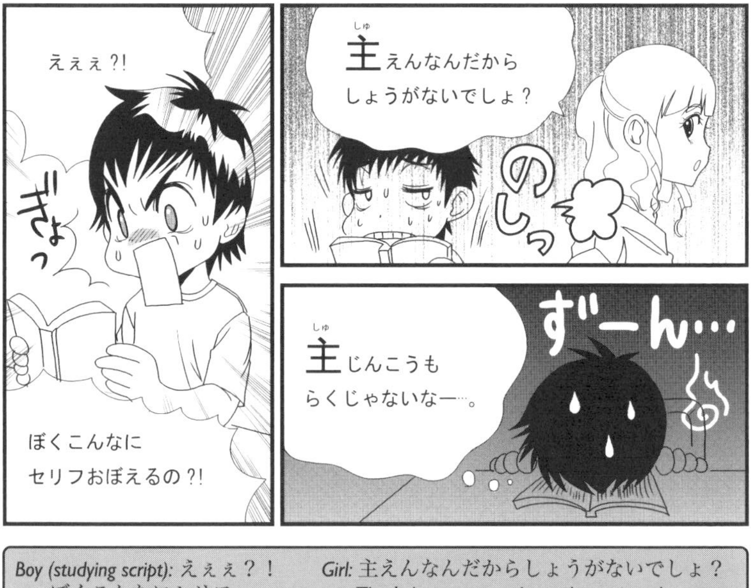
ええぇ?!
ぎょっ
ぼくこんなに
セリフおぼえるの?!
しゅ
主えんなんだから
しょうがないでしょ?
のしっ
しゅ
主じんこうも
らくじゃないなー…。
ずーん…

Boy (studying script): ええぇ？！
ぼくこんなにセリフ
おぼえるの？！
Whaaat?! I'm expected to memorize all of these lines?!

ぎょっ (sound of fear)

Girl: 主えんなんだからしょうがないでしょ？
That's because you have the main role, so no problem, right?

のしっ (sound of heavy stress)

Boy: 主じんこうもらくじゃないなー…。
It's not easy being a hero...

ずーん… (sound of depression)

HEAVY

おも(い)、かさ(ねる)、ジュウ、チョウ

ex. 重い (おもい) - heavy

ex. 慎重* (しんちょう) - carefulness

ex. 体重 (たいじゅう) - one's (body) weight

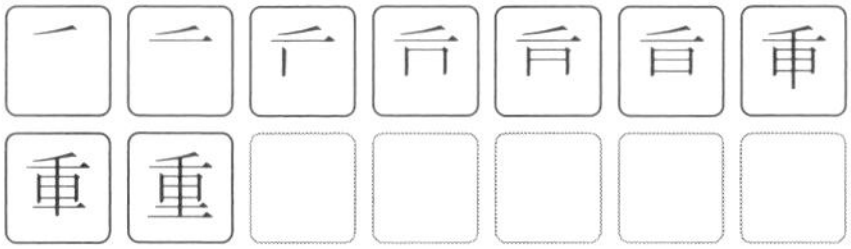

重

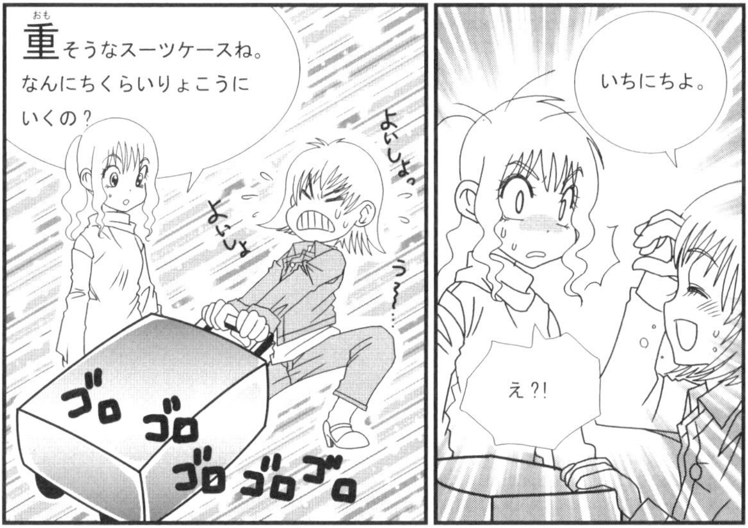

重そうなスーツケースね。なんにちくらいりょこうにいくの?
よいしょ
よいしょっ
う~…
ゴロ ゴロ ゴロ ゴロゴロ
いちにちよ。
え?!

Girl: 重そうなスーツケースね。
なんにちくらいりょこうにいくの?
Your suitcase looks heavy. How many days will you be away on your trip?

よいしょよいしょっ (sound of physical exertion)

うー… (sound made while pulling something)

ゴロゴロ (sound of something rolling)

Best friend: いちにちよ。
One day.

Girl: え?!
Huh?!

親

PARENTS / RELATIVES

おや、した(しい)、した(しむ)、シン

ex. 親子 (おやこ) - parent and child
ex. 親切 (しんせつ) - kindness
ex. 両親* (りょうしん) - parents

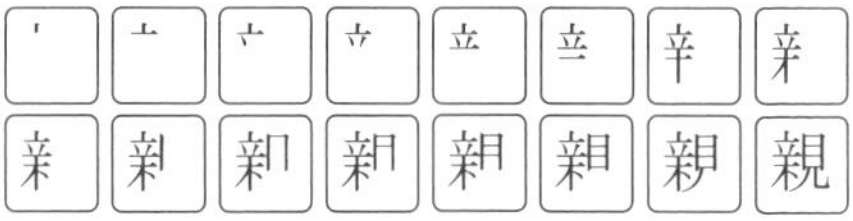

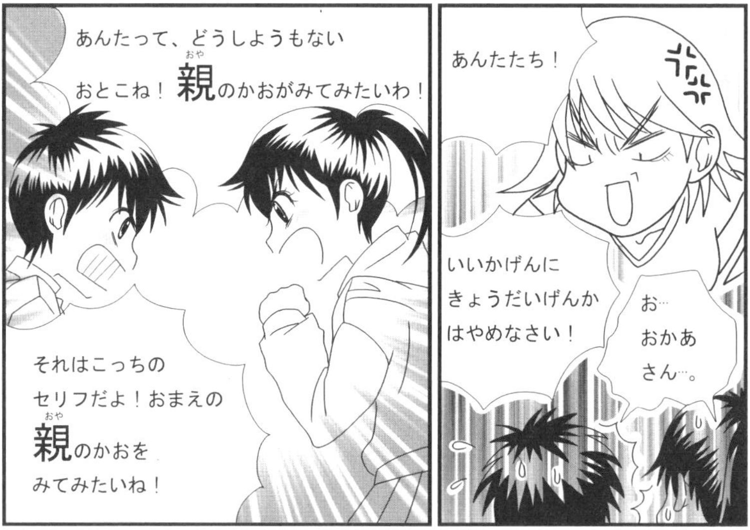
あんたって、どうしようもない
おとこね！親(おや)のかおがみてみたいわ！
それはこっちの
セリフだよ！おまえの
親(おや)のかおを
みてみたいね！
あんたたち！
いいかげんに
きょうだいげんか
はやめなさい！
お…
おかあ
さん…。

Girl: あんたって、どうしようもないおとこね！
親のかおがみてみたいわ！
What a pathetic little man you are!
I would love to talk to your parents about it!

Boy: それはこっちのセリフだよ！
おまえの親のかおをみてみたいね！
That's my line! I want to talk to *your* parents!

Mother: あんたたち！
いいかげんにきょうだいげんかはやめなさい！
You two! Stop fighting! you are brother and sister!

Both: お…　おかあさん…。
M... Mother...

WORLD / BOUNDS

カイ

ex. 魔界* (まかい) - world of evil spirits; hell
ex. 限界* (げんかい) - limit
ex. 視界* (しかい) - view, sight

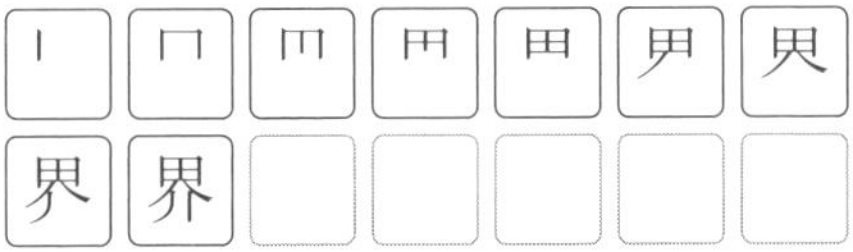

界

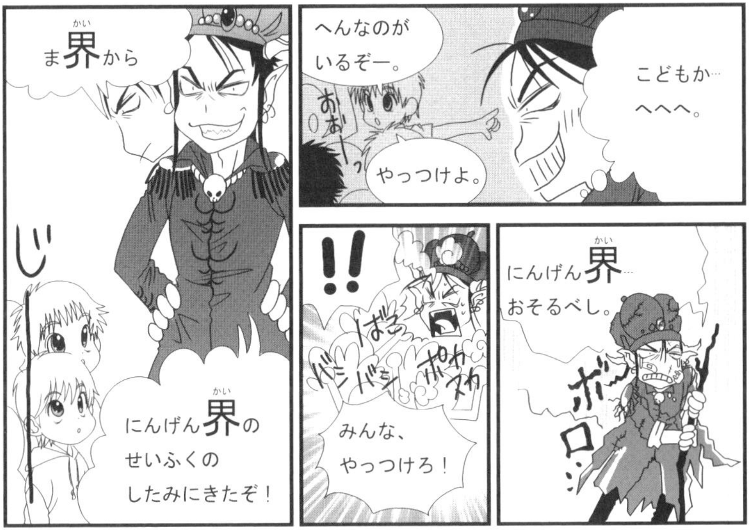

ま界(かい)から
にんげん界(かい)のせいふくのしたみにきたぞ！
じ
へんなのがいるぞー。
おおーっ
やっつけよ。
こどもか…へへへ。
!!
ばこ
バシバシ
ポカスカ
みんな、やっつけろ！
にんげん界(かい)…おそるべし。
ボロ…

Devil: ま界から にんげん界のせいふくのしたみにきたぞ！ I came from the world of evil spirits to the human world for a quick look before I conquer you all!
Children: じー (staring)
Children: へんなのがいるぞー。 What a weirdo. やっつけよ。 Let's get him. おおーっ Yeah!
Devil: こどもか… へへへ。 Children... Heh-heh-heh.
Children: みんな、やっつけろ！ Everyone, beat him up!
ばこ バシバシ ポカスカ (slapping, punching, kicking)
Devil: にんげん界… おそるべし。 The human world is a scary place.
ボロ… (worn out)

貸

LEND

か(す)、タイ

ex. 貸す (かす) - to lend

ex. 賃貸* (ちんたい) - rental; lease

ex. 貸借 (たいしゃく) - debit and credit

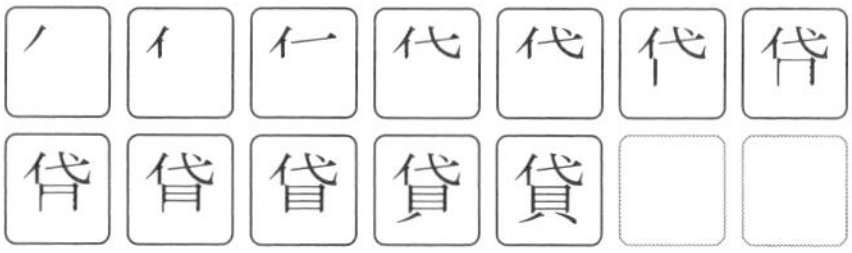

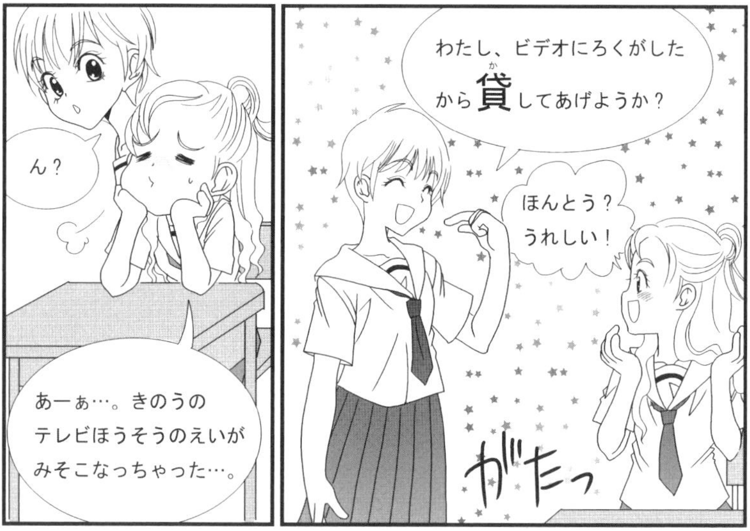
ん？
あーぁ…。きのうのテレビほうそうのえいがみそこなっちゃった…。
わたし、ビデオにろくがしたから貸(か)してあげようか？
ほんとう？うれしい！
がたっ

Schoolgirl at desk: あーぁ…。
きのうのテレビほうそうのえいがみそこなっちゃった…。
Sigh... I missed the movie on TV yesterday...

Classmate: ん？
Huh?

Classmate: わたし、ビデオにろくがしたから貸してあげようか？
I recorded it on videotape...shall I lend it to you?

Schoolgirl at desk: ほんとう？うれしい！
Really? I'm so happy!

がたっ (sound of a chair being pushed back)

PASS

かよ(う)、とお(る)、ツウ

ex. 通る (とおる) - to pass along
ex. 通う (かよう) - to commute
ex. 通訳* (つうやく) - interpreter

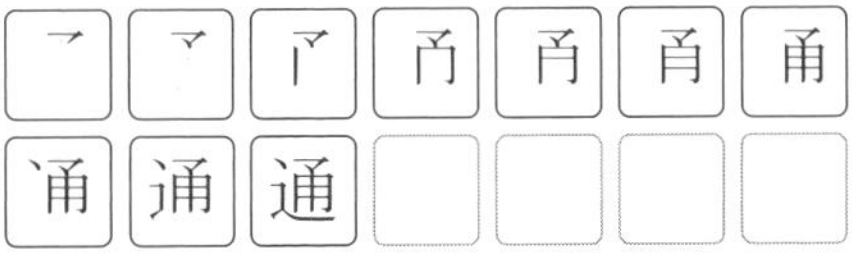

通

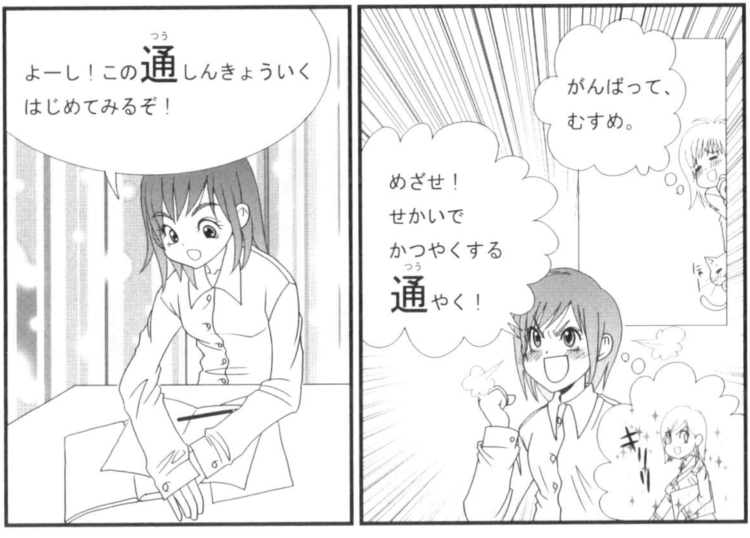
よーし！この通しんきょういく
はじめてみるぞ！
がんばって、
むすめ。
めざせ！
せかいで
かつやくする
通やく！
キリリ

Teenage girl: よーし！
この通しんきょういく
はじめてみるぞ！
All right! I'm going to try
this correspondence course!

Teenage girl: めざせ！せかいでかつやく
する通やく！
Aim high! An interpreter who flourishes
all across the world!

キリリ (looking sharp)

Mother: がんばって、むすめ。That's my girl.

にゃー (cat's meow)

体

BODY

からだ、タイ

ex. 体力 (たいりょく) - physical strength
ex. 体育* (たいいく) - gymnastics
ex. 体調* (たいちょう) - health condition

ノ	亻	仁	什	伙	休	体

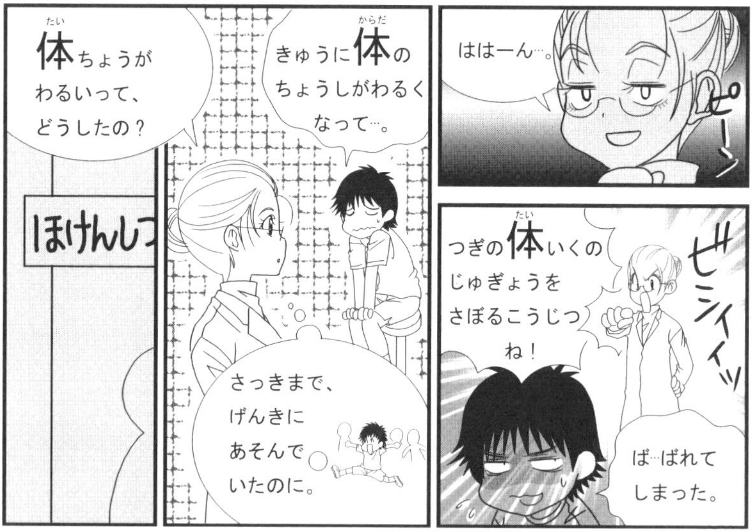
体ちょうがわるいって、どうしたの？
ほけんしつ
きゅうに体のちょうしがわるくなって…。
さっきまで、げんきにあそんでいたのに。
ははーん…。
ピーン
つぎの体いくのじゅぎょうをさぼるこうじつね！
ビシイイッ
ば…ばれてしまった。

Door sign: ほけんしつ School infirmary
Nurse: 体ちょうがわるいって、どうしたの？
You are not feeling well? What's wrong?
Boy: きゅうに体のちょうしがわるくなって…。
I became sick all of a sudden...
Nurse: さっきまで、げんきにあそんでいたのに。
But you were playing just a moment ago.
Nurse: ははーん…。I get it...
ピーン (sound of realization)
Nurse: つぎの体いくのじゅぎょうをさぼるこうじつね！
Your trying to cut gym class!
ビシイイッ (sound of pointing)
Boy: ば…ばれてしまった。
B...Busted.

BORROW

か(りる)、シャク

ex. 借りる (かりる) - to borrow
ex. 借地人 (しゃくちにん) - tenant
ex. 借金 (しゃっきん) - loan

| Sister: | こんなにほんをもって、 どこにいくの？ Where are you going with all those books? | Brother: | としょかんで借りたほんを かえしにいくところなんだ。 I'm going to return the books I borrowed from the library. |
| Brother: | あぁ、このほん？ Oh, these books? | Sister: | わたしもとしょかんに ほんを借りにいってみよう。 I should go to the library to borrow some books too. |

代

SUBSTITUTE / PRICE

か(わる)、よ、タイ、ダイ

ex. 代わる (かわる) - to take over
ex. 交代* (こうたい) - change; shift
ex. 代金 (だいきん) - price

ノ イ 仁 代 代

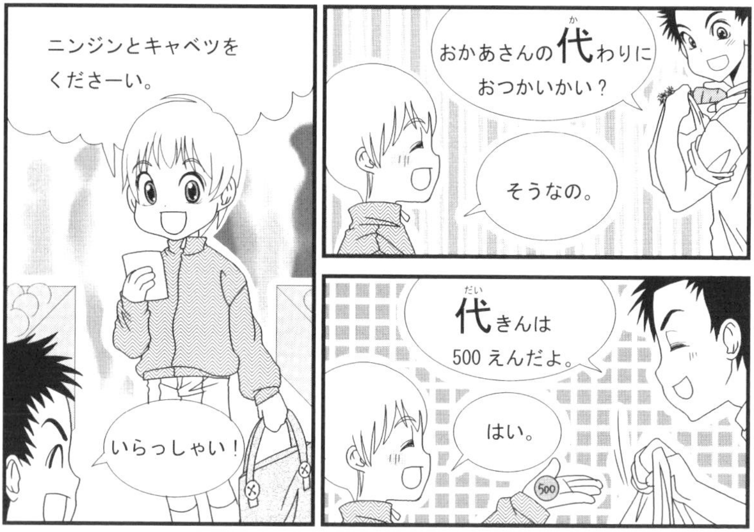
ニンジンとキャベツをくださーい。
いらっしゃい！
おかあさんの代わりにおつかいかい？
そうなの。
代きんは500えんだよ。
はい。
500

Vendor: いらっしゃい！
May I help you?

Boy: ニンジンとキャベツをくださーい。
May I have a carrot and cabbage please?

Vendor: おかあさんの代わりにおつかいかい？
So, you're shopping for your mother?

Boy: そうなの。That's right.

Vendor: 代きんは500えんだよ。
Your total comes to 500 yen.

Boy: はい。OK.

CHINESE

漢

カン

ex. 漢方薬 (かんぽうやく) - Chinese medicine
ex. 漢文 (かんぶん) - kanbun (Chinese writing)
ex. 大食漢 (たいしょくかん) - big eater

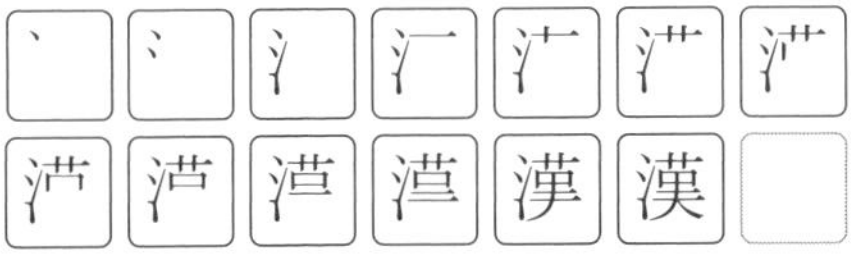

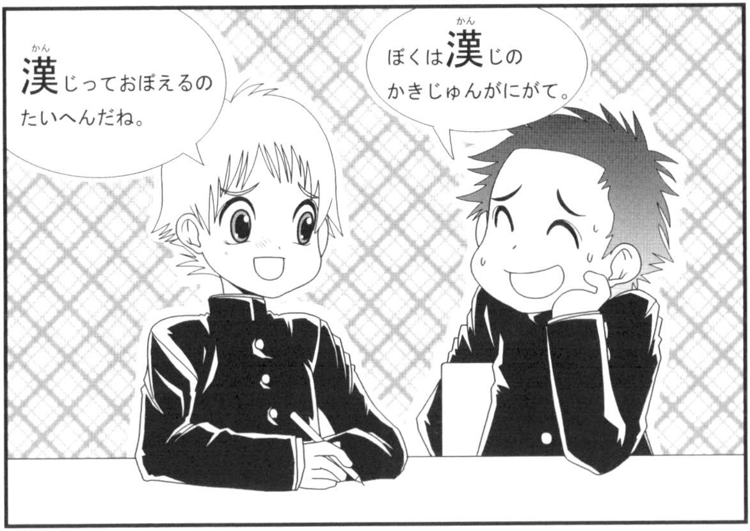
かん
漢じっておぼえるのたいへんだね。
かん
ぼくは漢じのかきじゅんがにがて。

Schoolboy on left: 漢じっておぼえるのたいへんだね。
Learning kanji is a lot of work.

Schoolboy on right: ぼくは漢じのかきじゅんがにがて。
I'm poor at the stroke orders of kanji.

館

BUILDING

カン

ex. 美術館* (びじゅつかん) - art museum
ex. 図書館 (としょかん) - library
ex. 旅館 (りょかん) - Japanese-style hotel

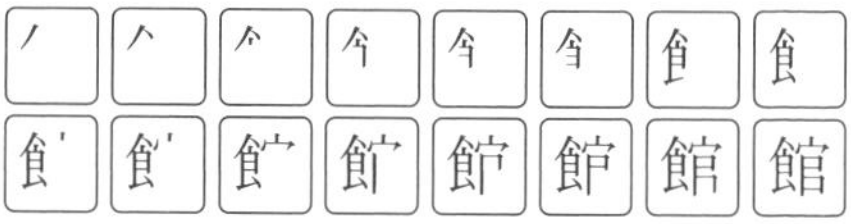

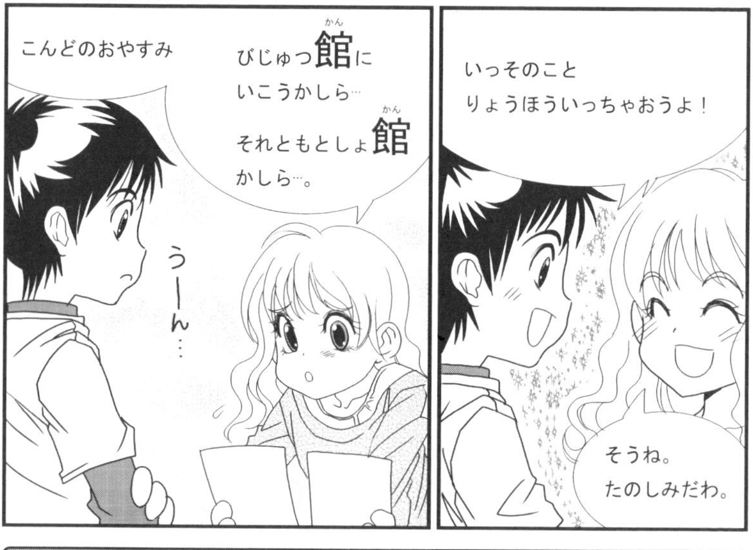
こんどのおやすみ
びじゅつ館にいこうかしら…
それともとしょ館かしら…。
うーん…
いっそのこと
りょうほういっちゃおうよ！
そうね。
たのしみだわ。

Girlfriend: こんどのおやすみ
びじゅつ館にいこうかしら…
それともとしょ館かしら…。
On our next day off, shall we go to the art museum... or the library?

Boyfriend: うーん…
Hmm...

Boyfriend: いっそのこと
りょうほういっちゃおうよ！
Why don't we go to both of them?

Girlfriend: そうね。たのしみだわ。
Right. That will be fun.

EXHAUSTIVE STUDY

キュウ

ex. 究極* (きゅうきょく) - ultimate
ex. 研究 (けんきゅう) - study; research
ex. 追究* (ついきゅう) - investigation

究

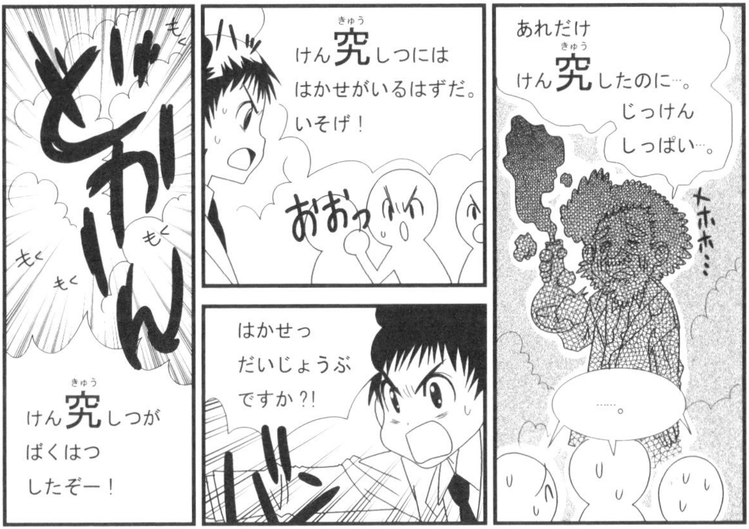
どかーん
もく
もく
もく
もく
けん究しつが
ばくはつ
したぞー！
ハッ
けん究しつには
はかせがいるはずだ。
いそげ！
おおっ
はかせっ
だいじょうぶ
ですか？!
あれだけ
けん究したのに…。
じっけん
しっぱい…。
トホホ…
……。

どかーん Boom! もくもく (sound of smoke rising) *Man:* けん究しつが ばくはつしたぞー! The laboratory has exploded!	ハッ (regaining consciousness) *Man:* けん究しつにははかせが いるはずだ。いそげ! The doctor is still in the lab. Hurry! *Rescuer:* おおっ Oh! バン (sound of door being thrown open) *Man:* はかせっだいじょうぶ ですか!? Doctor, are you OK?!	*Doctor:* あれだけ けん究したのに…。 じっけんしっぱい…。 Despite our exhaustive study... the experiment has failed. トホホ… (disappointed) *Rescuers:* (speechless)

業

WORK / INDUSTRY

ギョウ

ex. 産業* (さんぎょう) - industry
ex. 授業* (じゅぎょう) - lesson
ex. 卒業* (そつぎょう) - graduation

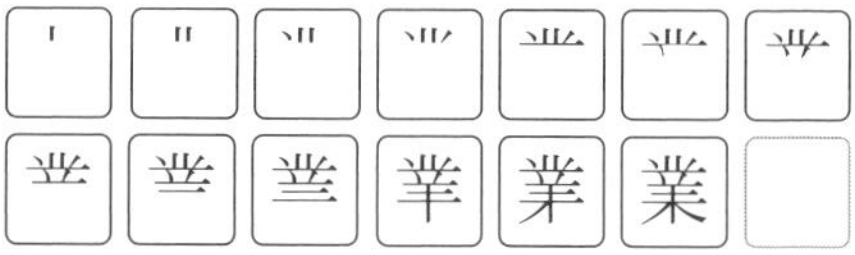

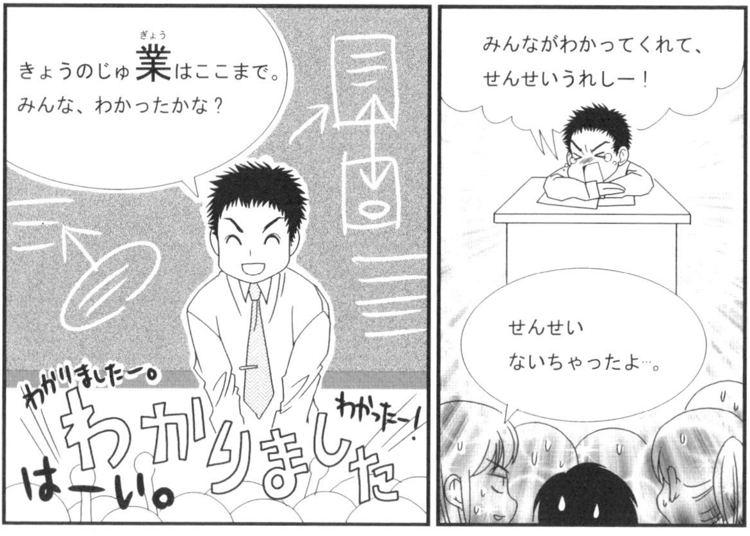
きょうのじゅ業はここまで。
みんな、わかったかな？
わかりましたー。
わかったー！
はーい。
わかりました
みんながわかってくれて、
せんせいうれしー！
せんせい
ないちゃったよ…。

Teacher: きょうのじゅ業はここまで。
みんな、わかったかな？
That's our lesson for today. Did everyone understand?

Students: わかりましたー。 We got it.
わかったー！ Understood!
はーい。 Yes, sir.
わかりました We understand.

Teacher (sobbing): みんながわかってくれて、
せんせいうれしー！
I'm so happy that everyone understood me!

Student: せんせい
ないちゃったよ…。
We made our teacher cry...

WEAR / ARRIVE

き(る)、つ(く)、チャク

ex. 着る (きる) - to wear

ex. 着く (つく) - to arrive

ex. 着席* (ちゃくせき) - sitting

| 丶 | ﾂ | 半 | 半 | 羊 | 羊 | 芏 |
| 芏 | 着 | 着 | 着 | 着 | | |

First girl: わっ！きれーい。

Wow! How pretty.

着ものなんか着てなにか
あったの？

What are you wearing your
kimono for?

Second girl: きょう、せいじんしきだから
着もの着てみたの。

I'm wearing my kimono for my
Coming-of-Age ceremony* today.

First girl: よくにあってるよ。

It looks great on you.

*Coming-of-Age Day – 成人の日 (せいじんのひ) – is a Japanese holiday for 20-year-olds held annually on the second Monday of January. Female participants wear long-sleeved kimono called 振り袖 (ふりそで) on this day.

銀

SILVER

ギン

ex. 銀貨* (ぎんか) - silver coin

ex. 銀行 (ぎんこう) - bank

ex. 銀世界 (ぎんせかい) - snowscape

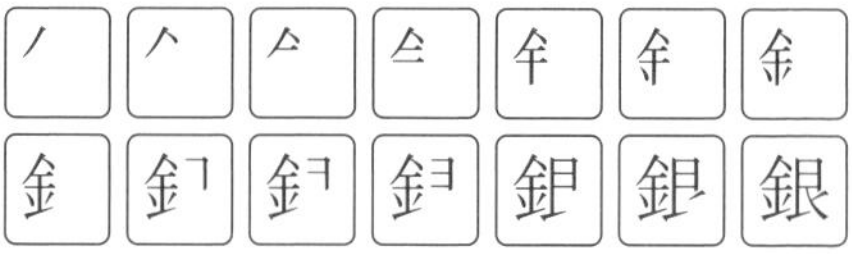

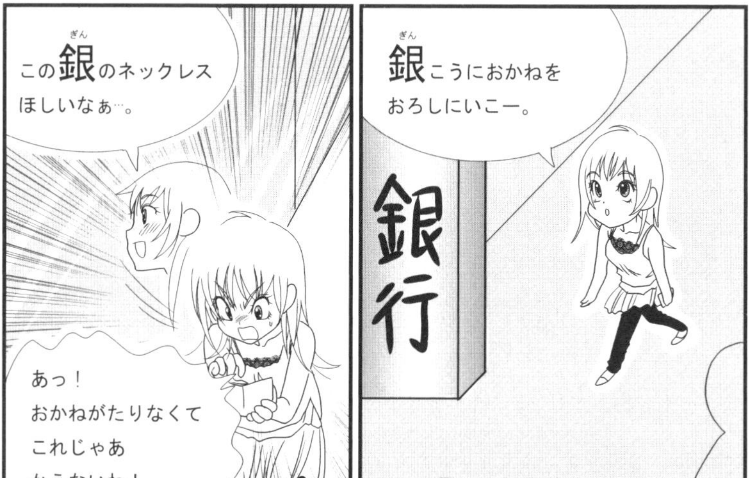
ぎん
この銀のネックレス
ほしいなぁ…。
あっ！
おかねがたりなくて
これじゃあ
かえないわ！
ぎん
銀こうにおかねを
おろしにいこー。
銀行

Girl: この銀のネックレスほしいなぁ…。
I really want this silver necklace.

あっ！おかねがたりなくて
これじゃあかえないわ！
Darn! I don't have enough money
to buy it!

銀こうにおかねをおろしにいこー。
It's off to the bank to borrow some cash.

Sign: 銀行 (ぎんこう) - bank

GRIND / RESEARCH

ケン

ex. 研究所* (けんきゅうじょ) - laboratory
ex. 研修* (けんしゅう) - training
ex. 研磨* (けんま) - polish

一	厂	丆	石	石	石	矴
研	研					

きょうで研しゅうもおわり。これでやっと、いちにんまえの研きゅういんだね。

やっとだね。

これからもっとじぶんを研ましなくちゃな。

よーし。

わたしもがんばるぞ。

Young man: きょうで研しゅうもおわり。
これでやっと、いちにんまえの
研きゅういんだね。
Today is the final day of training.
I'm now a lab researcher.

Young woman: やっとだね。
Finally.

Young man: これからもっと
じぶんを研ましなくちゃな。
I still have to continue training
for the future on my own.

Young woman: よーし。わたしも
がんばるぞ。
All right. I will try my best too.

験

TEST

ケン

ex. 試験 (しけん) - test; exam
ex. 受験* (じゅけん) - taking an examination
ex. 経験* (けいけん) - experience

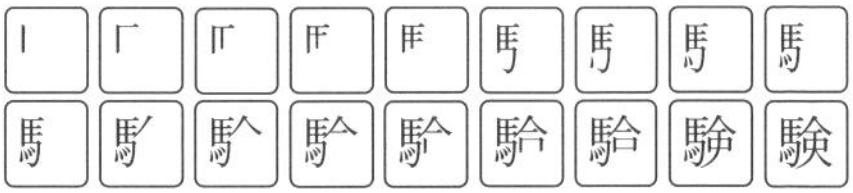

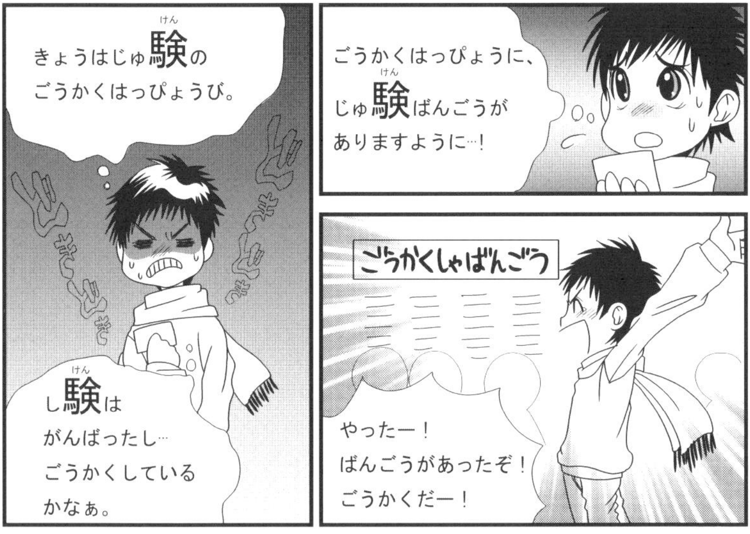
きょうはじゅ験の
ごうかくはっぴょうび。
どきどき
どきどき
し験は
がんばったし…
ごうかくしている
かなぁ。
ごうかくはっぴょうに、
じゅ験ばんごうが
ありますように…!
ごうかくしゃばんごう
やったー!
ばんごうがあったぞ!
ごうかくだー!

Student: きょうはじゅ験の
ごうかくはっぴょうび。
The results of the entrance exam will be announced today.
し験はがんばったし…
ごうかくしているかなぁ。
I did my best for the test...
I hope I passed. どきどき (heartbeat)
ごうかくはっぴょうに、
じゅ験ばんごうがありますように…!
I pray my number is on the bulletin board showing those who passed!
Sign: ごうかくしゃばんごう (Successful Applicants)
やったー!ばんごうがあったぞ!
ごうかくだー! Yeah! My number is there!
I passed!

TRY

試

こころ(みる)、シ

ex. 試みる (こころみる) - to try
ex. 試走 (しそう) - test drive; trial run
ex. 試行錯誤*(しこうさくご) - trial-and-error

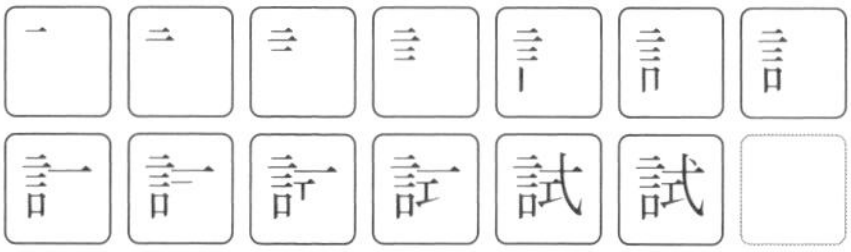

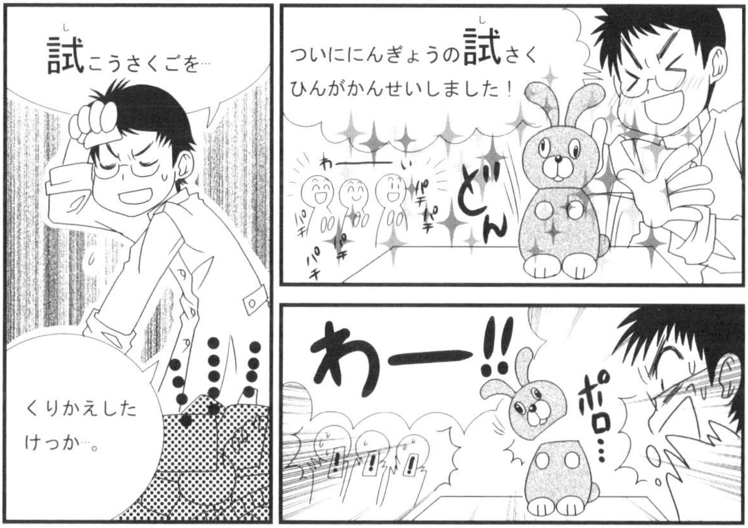
試こうさくごを…
くりかえした
けっか…。
ついににんぎょうの試さく
ひんがかんせいしました！
わーーい
パチ
パチ
どん
わー!!
ポロ…

Inventor: 試こうさくごを…
くりかえしたけっか…。
After several rounds of trial-and-error...

Inventor: ついににんぎょうの試さく
ひんがかんせいしました！
The trial version of this doll is finally ready!

Employees (in unison): わーい Yeah!

パチパチ (clap clap) どん (bang)

ポロ (sound of the head of the doll popping off)

Inventor: わー！！ Ugh!!

事

CHARGE / AFFAIR

こと、ジ

ex. 仕事 (しごと) - work
ex. 事々* (ことごと) - everything
ex. 事実* (じじつ) - fact

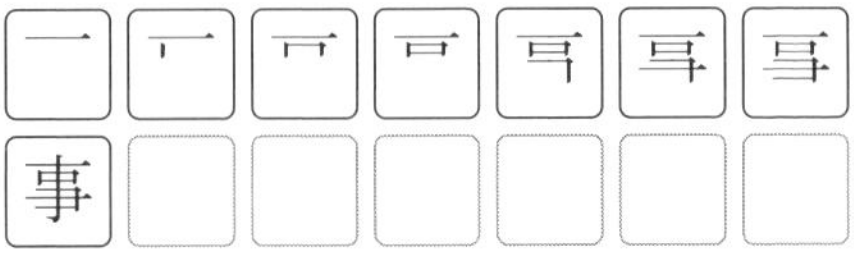

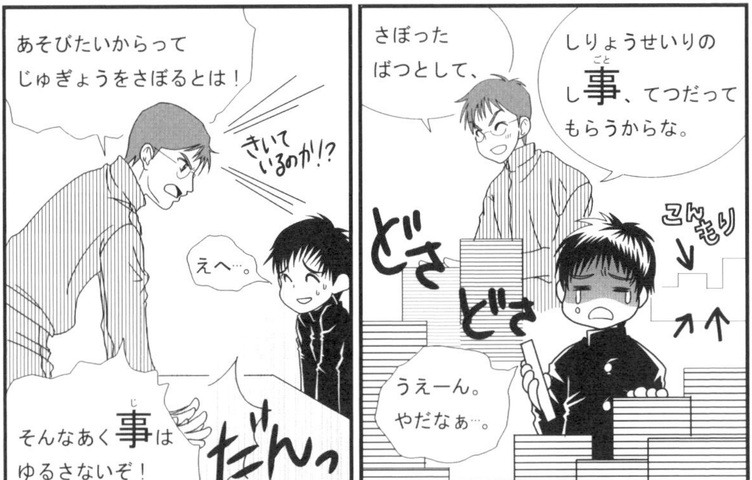
あそびたいからって
じゅぎょうをさぼるとは！
きいているのか!?
えへ…。
そんなあく事は
ゆるさないぞ！
だんっ
さぼった
ばつとして、
しりょうせいりの
し事、てつだって
もらうからな。
こんもり
どさ
どさ
うえーん。
やだなぁ…。

Teacher: あそびたいからって
じゅぎょうをさぼるとは！
Skipping lessons to go out and play!
きいているのか！？Are you listening!?
Student: えへ…。 Um...
Teacher: そんなあく事はゆるさないぞ！
I won't allow such behavior!
だんっ (slam)
Teacher: さぼったばつとして、
しりょうせいりのし事、てつだって
もらうからな。
You're under detention and will help me
with my work.
こんもり (a pile of documents)
どさどさ (sound of documents piling up)
Student: うえーん。やだなぁ…。Wah. Ugh...

TURN

ころ(がる)、ころ(げる)、テン

ex. 転がる (ころがる) - to roll over
ex. 回転* (かいてん) - rotation
ex. 転倒* (てんとう) - tumble

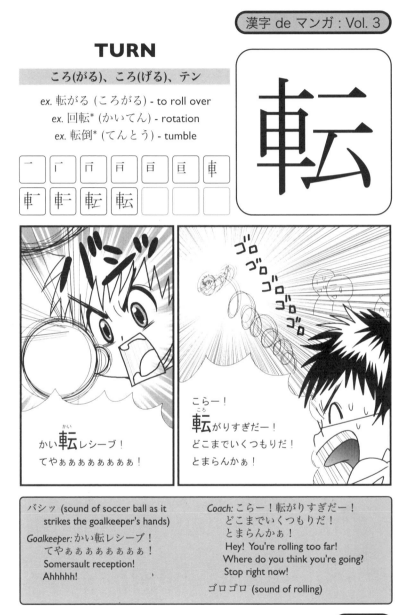

かい転レシーブ！
てやぁぁぁぁぁぁぁぁ！

こらー！
転がりすぎだー！
どこまでいくつもりだ！
とまらんかぁ！

バシッ (sound of soccer ball as it strikes the goalkeeper's hands)

Goalkeeper: かい転レシーブ！
てやぁぁぁぁぁぁぁぁ！
Somersault reception!
Ahhhhh!

Coach: こらー！転がりすぎだー！
どこまでいくつもりだ！
とまらんかぁ！
Hey! You're rolling too far!
Where do you think you're going?
Stop right now!

ゴロゴロ (sound of rolling)

LEAVE / GO AWAY

さ(る)、キョ、コ

ex. 去る (さる) - to leave
ex. 過去* (かこ) - the past
ex. 去年 (きょねん) - last year

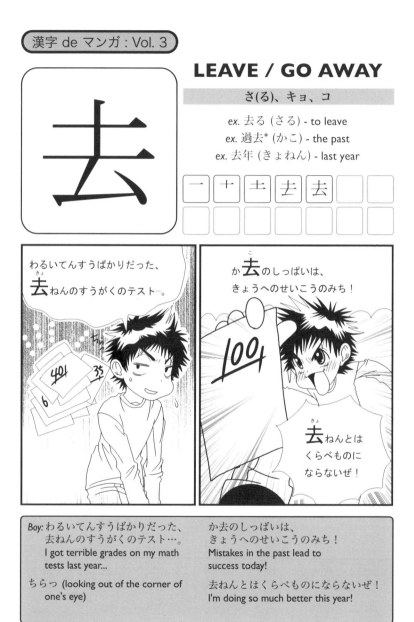

Boy: わるいてんすうばかりだった、去ねんのすうがくのテスト…。 I got terrible grades on my math tests last year...	か去のしっぱいは、きょうへのせいこうのみち！ Mistakes in the past lead to success today!
ちらっ (looking out of the corner of one's eye)	去ねんとはくらべものにならないぜ！ I'm doing so much better this year!

QUALITY

質

シツ

ex. 質問 (しつもん) - question
ex. 素質* (そしつ) - capability
ex. 品質* (ひんしつ) - quality

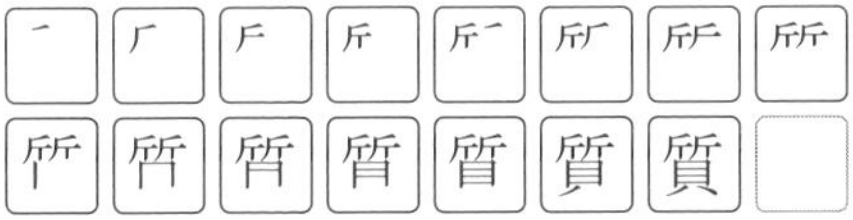

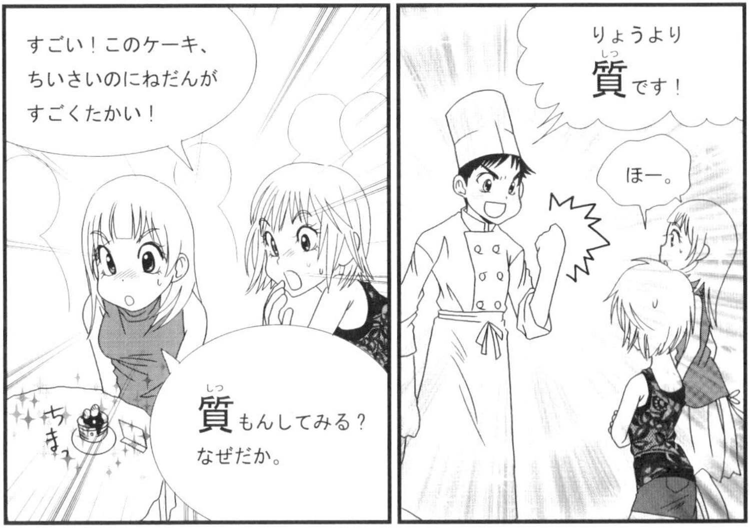
すごい！このケーキ、
ちいさいのにねだんが
すごくたかい！
質(しつ)もんしてみる？
なぜだか。
ちまっ
りょうより
質(しつ)です！
ほー。

First girl (on right): すごい！このケーキ、ちいさいのにねだんがすごくたかい！
Wow! For something so small, this cake sure is expensive!

Second girl: 質もんしてみる？なぜだか。
Shall we ask why?

ちまっ (sound representing something neat and compact)

Chef: りょうより質です！
Quality before quantity!

Girls (in unison): ほー。
Ahhh...

品

ARTICLE / QUALITY

しな、ヒン

ex. 品物 (しなもの) - goods
ex. 上品 (じょうひん) - elegance
ex. 食品 (しょくひん) - foodstuff

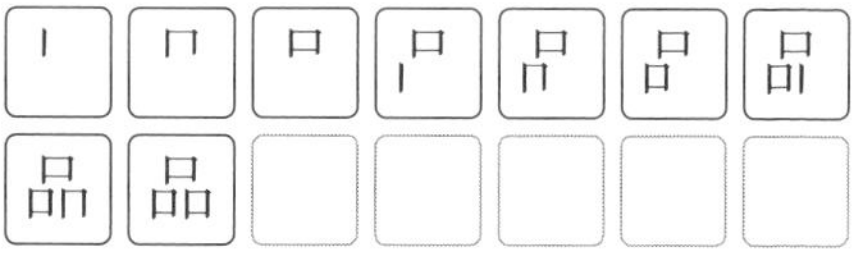

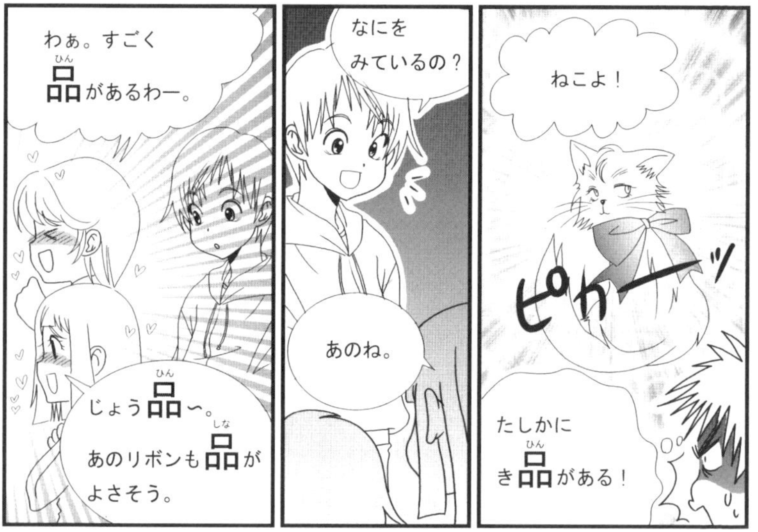

わぁ。すごく品(ひん)があるわー。
じょう品(ひん)〜。あのリボンも品(しな)がよさそう。
なにをみているの？
あのね。
ねこよ！
ピカーッ
たしかにき品(ひん)がある！

First girl: わぁ。すごく品があるわー。
Wow. It looks so elegant.

Second girl: じょう品〜。あのリボンも品がよさそう。
How graceful. That ribbon must be high-quality, too.

Boy: なにをみているの？
What are you looking at?

Second girl: あのね。
Well...

Second girl: ねこよ！
It's a cat!

Boy: たしかにき品がある！
It certainly is elegant!

ピカーッ (beautiful glow)

DIE

し(ぬ)、シ

ex. 死ぬ (しぬ) - to die
ex. 必死* (ひっし) - desperation
ex. 死亡* (しぼう) - death

一	厂	歹	歹	歹	死	

死

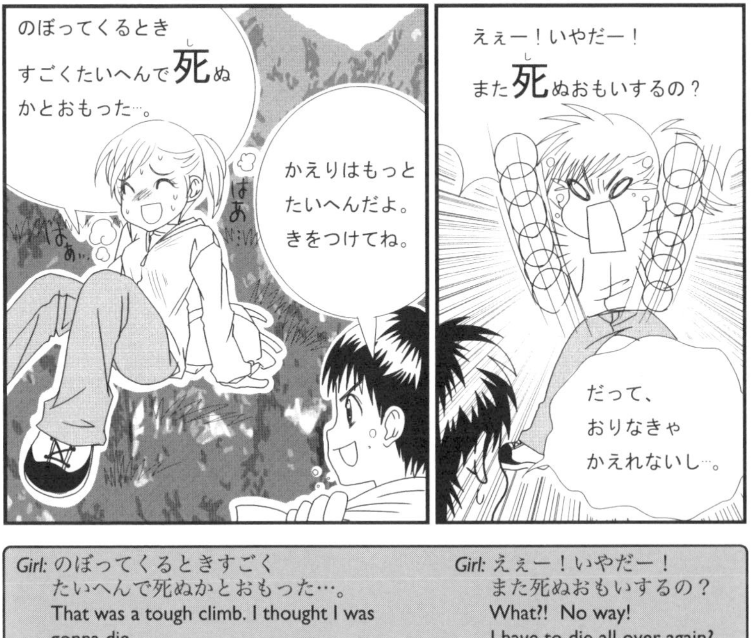
のぼってくるときすごくたいへんで死ぬかとおもった…。
はぁ…
はあ
かえりはもっとたいへんだよ。きをつけてね。
えぇー！いやだー！また死ぬおもいするの？
だって、おりなきゃかえれないし…。

Girl: のぼってくるときすごくたいへんで死ぬかとおもった…。
That was a tough climb. I thought I was gonna die...
はあはあ (pant pant)
Boy: かえりはもっとたいへんだよ。きをつけてね。
It's even harder the way back. Be careful.

Girl: えぇー！いやだー！また死ぬおもいするの？
What?! No way!
I have to die all over again?
Boy: だって、おりなきゃかえれないし…。
But we have to climb down to go home...

DRAWING

ズ、ト

ex. 地図 (ちず) - map
ex. 図画工作 (ずがこうさく) - arts and crafts
ex. 設計図* (せっけいず) - plan; blueprint

| 丨 | 冂 | 冈 | 冈 | 図 | 図 | 図 |

Teacher: このち図からよみとれる
ふうけいをそうぞうして
かいてみようねー。
Using this map, let's draw an
imaginary landscape.

Students (in unison): はーい
Ye-esssss!

Girl: どうしたの？
What's the matter?

Boy; 図がこうさくって
にがてなんだよねー…。
I'm terrible at arts and crafts...

LIVE / RESIDE

す(まう)、す(む)、ジュウ

ex. 住む (すむ) - to live in
ex. 住所* (じゅうしょ) - address
ex. 住民* (じゅうみん) - residents

住

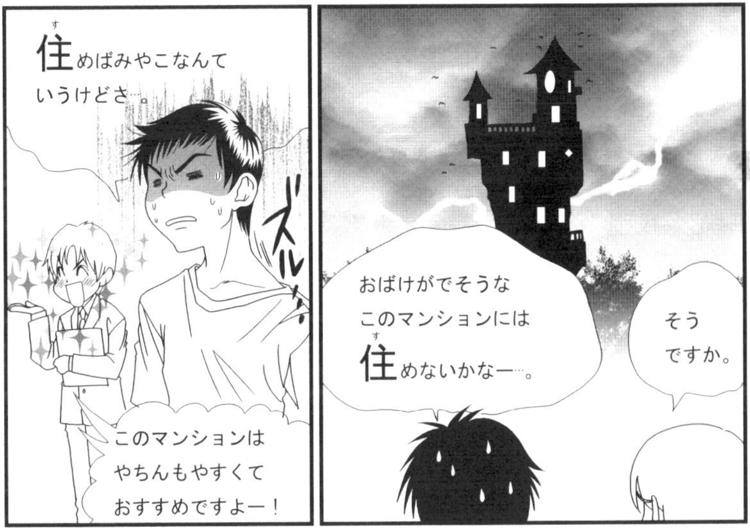
住めばみやこなんていうけどさ…。
ズル…
このマンションはやちんもやすくておすすめですよー！
おばけがでそうなこのマンションには住めないかなー…。
そうですか。

Man: 住めばみやこなんていうけどさ…。
They say there's no place like home...
ズル… (sound of shirt slipping as man's shoulders slump in surprise)
Real estate agent: このマンションは やちんもやすくて おすすめですよー！
This place comes highly recommended, and the rent is quite low!
Man: おばけがでそうな このマンションには 住めないかなー…。
But I don't think I can live in a haunted house...
Real estate agent: そうですか。
If you say so.

族

FAMILY

ゾク

ex. 水族館 (すいぞくかん) - aquarium
ex. 暴走族 (ぼうそうぞく) - hot-rod gang
ex. 民族* (みんぞく) - nation

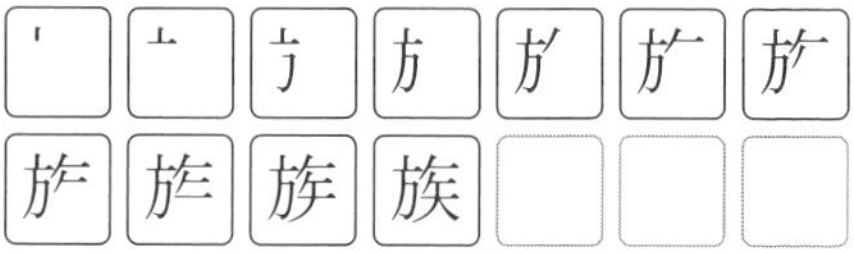

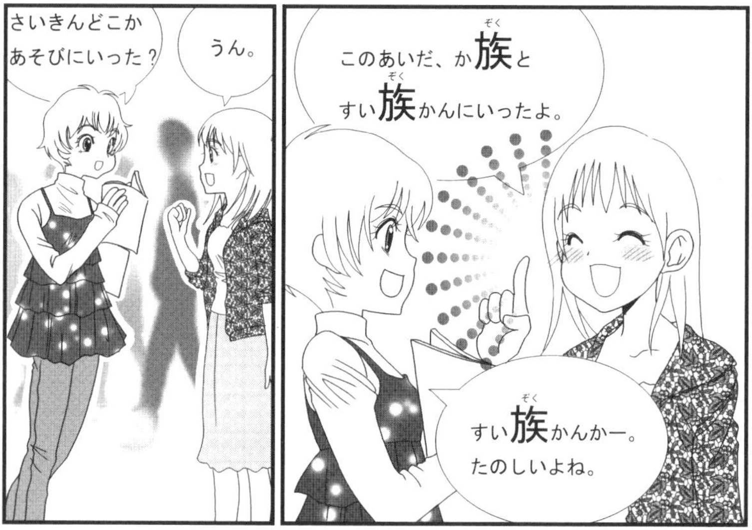
さいきんどこか あそびにいった？
うん。
このあいだ、か族(ぞく)と すい族(ぞく)かんにいったよ。
すい族(ぞく)かんかー。 たのしいよね。

Girl on left (holding travel guide): さいきんどこか あそびにいった？
Have you gone anywhere recently?

Girl on right: うん。
Yup.

Girl on right: このあいだ、か族と すい族かんにいったよ。
I went to the aquarium with my family the other day.

Girl on left: すい族かんかー。 たのしいよね。
The aquarium, huh? That's sounds like fun.

POUR / CONCENTRATE

そそ(ぐ)、チュウ

ex. 注ぐ (そそぐ) - to pour; to flow
ex. 注射 (ちゅうしゃ) - injection
ex. 注文 (ちゅうもん) - order

注

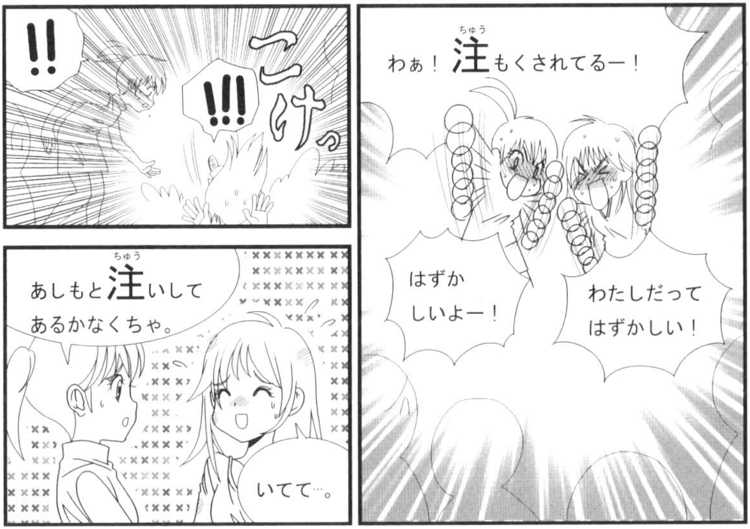
!!
!!!
こけっ
あしもと注いしてあるかなくちゃ。
いてて…。
わぁ！注もくされてるー！
はずかしいよー！
わたしだってはずかしい！

こけっ (tumble)

Girl on left: あしもと注いして あるかなくちゃ。
You should watch your step.

Girl on right: いてて…。
Ouch...

Girls (noticing everyone is watching them): わぁ！注もくされてるー！
Oh, no! We're the center of attention!

Girl on left: はずかしいよー！
I'm so embarrassed!

Girl on right: わたしだってはずかしい！
I'm embarrassed too!

題

TITLE

ダイ

ex. 題名 (だいめい) - title; task
ex. 宿題 (しゅくだい) - homework
ex. 話題 (わだい) - topic of conversation

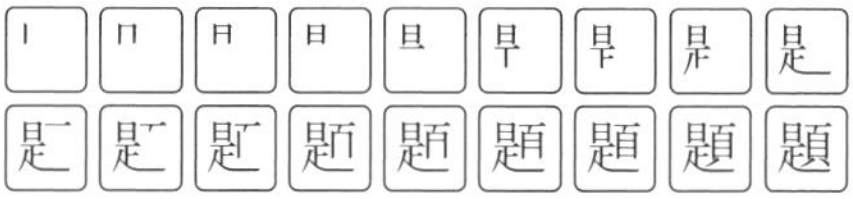

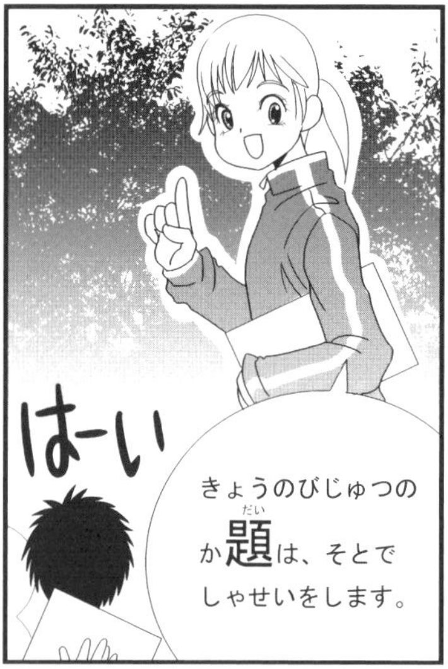
はーい
きょうのびじゅつのか題(だい)は、そとでしゃせいをします。

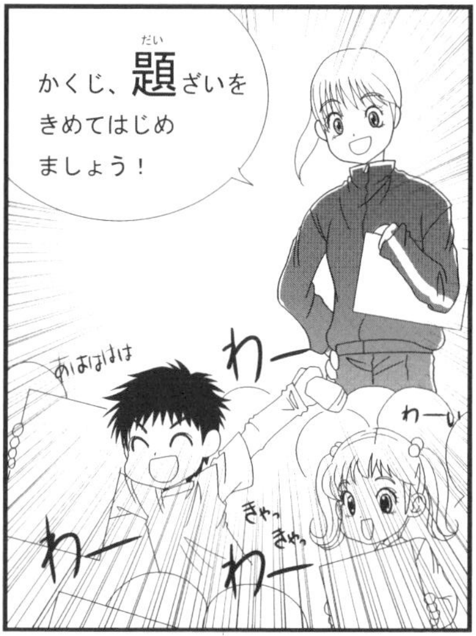
かくじ、題(だい)ざいをきめてはじめましょう！
あはははは
わー
わーい
きゃっきゃっ
わー
わー

Teacher: きょうのびじゅつのか題は、そとでしゃせいをします。
Today's art assignment is to go outdoors and make a sketch.

Students (in unison): はーい
Ye-esss!

Teacher: かくじ、題ざいをきめてはじめましょう！
Everyone, find your subject and begin!

Children: わー (cheering)
わーい Yay!
あははは (laughing)
きゃっきゃっ (giggling)

BUILD

た(つ)、た(てる)、ケン

ex. 建てる (たてる) - to build
ex. 建物 (たてもの) - a building
ex. 建築* (けんちく) - architecture

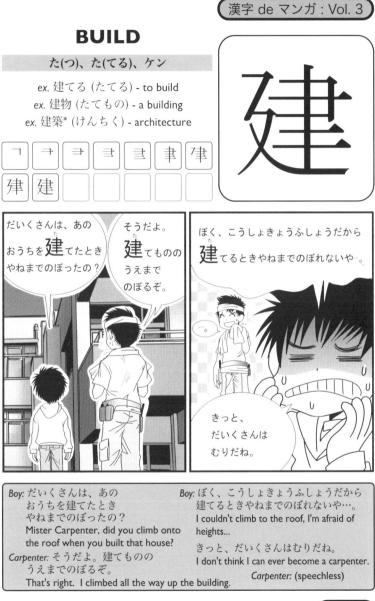

だいくさんは、あの
おうちを**建**てたとき
やねまでのぼったの？

そうだよ。
建てものの
うえまで
のぼるぞ。

ぼく、こうしょきょうふしょうだから
建てるときやねまでのぼれないや…。

きっと、
だいくさんは
むりだね。

Boy: だいくさんは、あの
おうちを建てたとき
やねまでのぼったの？
Mister Carpenter, did you climb onto
the roof when you built that house?

Carpenter: そうだよ。建てものの
うえまでのぼるぞ。
That's right. I climbed all the way up the building.

Boy: ぼく、こうしょきょうふしょうだから
建てるときやねまでのぼれないや…。
I couldn't climb to the roof, I'm afraid of
heights...

きっと、だいくさんはむりだね。
I don't think I can ever become a carpenter.
Carpenter: (speechless)

TRIP / TRAVEL

たび、リョ

ex. 船旅* (ふなたび) - voyage
ex. 旅券* (りょけん) - passport
ex. 旅行 (りょこう) - travel

Man: 旅がしたい…	Man: 旅がしたいよー！ ぱぁーっと！
I want to take a trip...	旅こうにいきたいよー！ 旅にでたいぞー！
ボソ… (muttering to himself)	I want to take a trip! To loosen up. I want to go on a trip! I want to travel!
	Boss: きみ…。しごとちゅうはさけばないようにね。
	Hey you... You aren't supposed to shout during work. オホンッ (ahem)
	Man: は…はい。つい…。 S... Sorry. It just came out...

USE

使

つか(う)、シ

ex. 使う (つかう) - to use
ex. 使用法* (しようほう) - usage
ex. 大使 (たいし) - ambassador

ノ	亻	仁	仁	佢	佢	使
使						

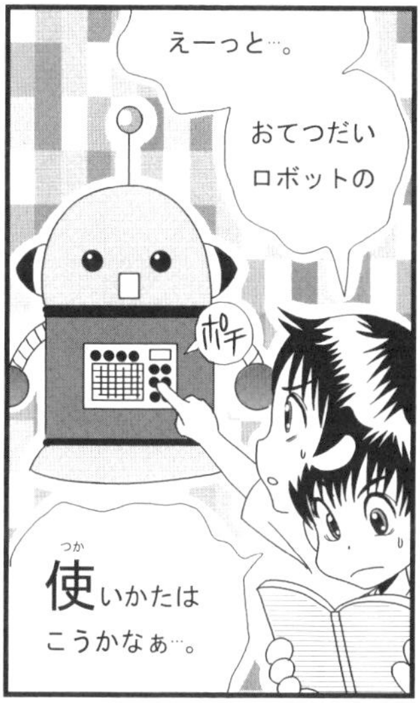
えーっと…。
おてつだい
ロボットの
ポチ
使いかたは
こうかなぁ…。

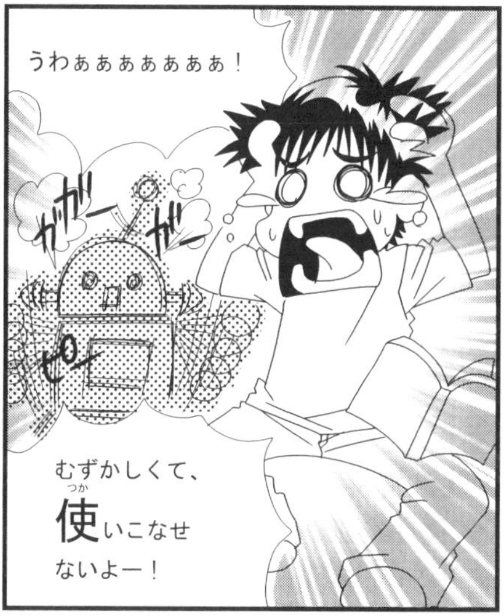
うわぁぁぁぁぁぁぁぁ！
ガガー
ガー
ピー
むずかしくて、
使いこなせ
ないよー！

Boy (reading manual): えーっと…。
おてつだいロボットの
使いかたはこうかなぁ…。
Hmmm...
How do I use this robot...?

ポチ (click)

Boy: うわぁぁぁぁぁぁぁぁ！
むずかしくて、使いこなせないよー！
Ugh! This is too hard. I'll never be able to use this perfectly.

ガーガーピー (sound of malfunctioning robot)

仕

SERVE / DO

つか(える)、シ

ex. 仕える (つかえる) - to serve
ex. 仕事場* (しごとば) - worksite
ex. 奉仕* (ほうし) - service

ノ	イ	仁	什	仕		

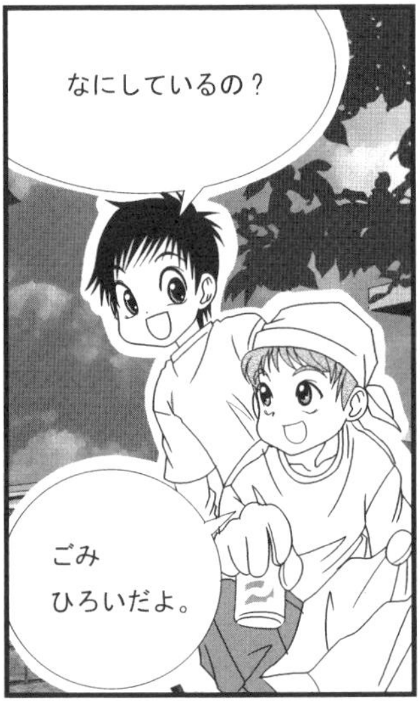
なにしているの？
ごみ
ひろいだよ。

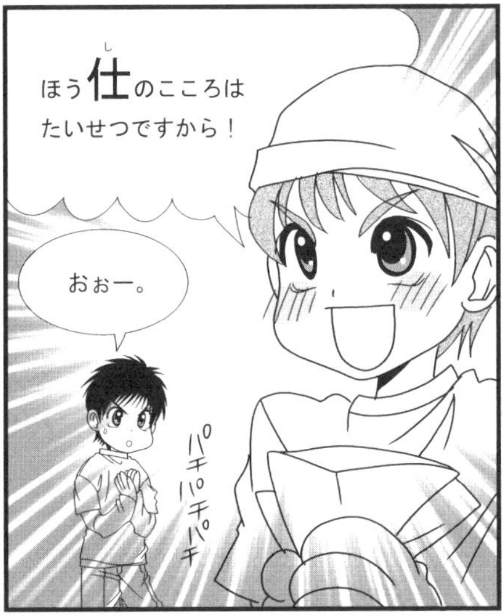
ほう仕のこころは
たいせつですから！
おぉー。
パチパチパチ

First boy: なにしているの？
What are you doing?

Second boy: ごみひろいだよ。
I'm picking up litter.

Second boy: ほう仕のこころは
たいせつですから！
Public service is righteous!

First boy: おぉー。
Woah...

パチパチパチ (sound of clapping)

DEGREE / TIME

度

ド

ex. 温度* (おんど) - temperature
ex. 角度* (かくど) - angle
ex. 速度* (そくど) - speed

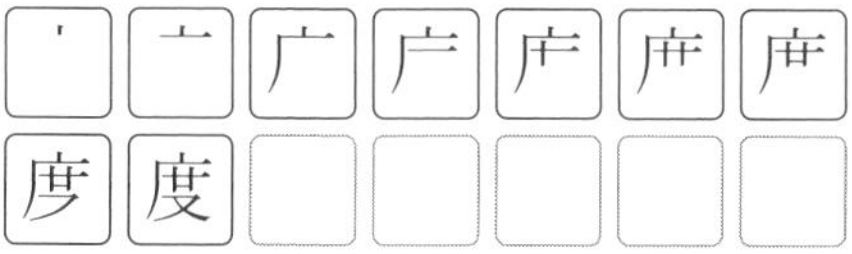

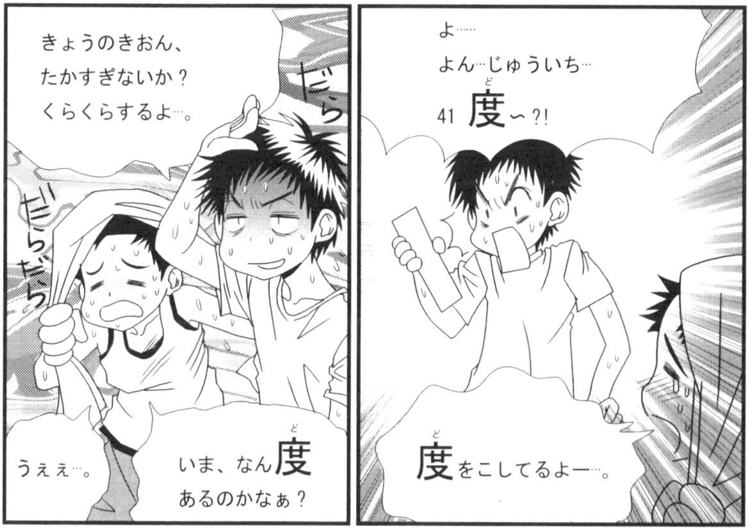

きょうのきおん、たかすぎないか？くらくらするよ…。
だら
だらだら
うぇぇ…。
いま、なん度あるのかなぁ？
よ……
よん…じゅういち…
41 度〜?!
度をこしてるよー…。

First boy: きょうのきおん、たかすぎないか？ くらくらするよ…。
Isn't today's temperature too high? I'm getting dizzy...
だらだら (sweat running down)

Second boy: うぇぇ…。いま、なん度あるのかなぁ？
Ugh... What is the temperature right now?

First boy: よ…よん…じゅういち…41度〜？！
Four... Forty-one... 41 degrees C*?!

Second boy: 度をこしてるよー…。
That's too high...

*41 degrees Celsius is about 106 F. Celsius is commonly used in Japan; Fahrenheit is almost never used.

問

QUESTION

と(い)、と(う)、とん、モン

ex. 問う（とう） - to ask; to question
ex. 問題（もんだい） - problem; question
ex. 問屋（とんや） - wholesale store

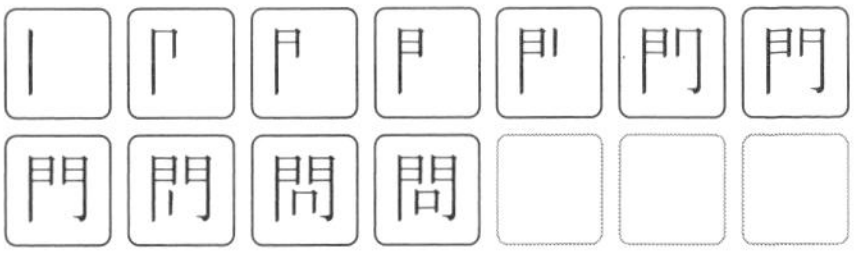

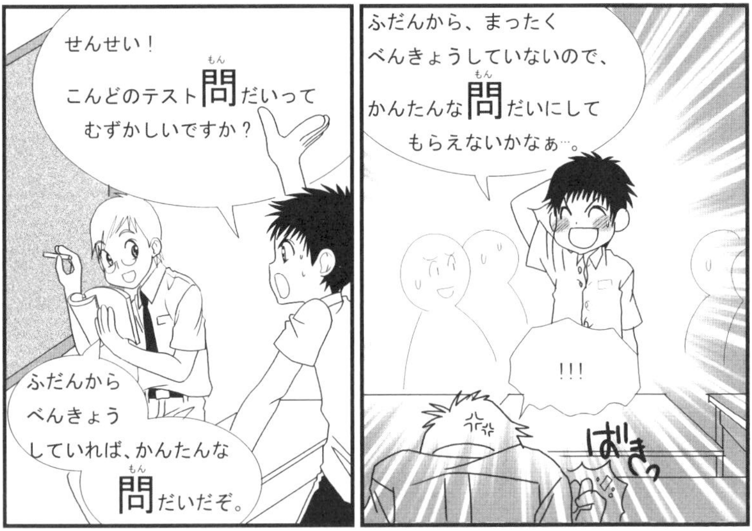
せんせい！
こんどのテスト問(もん)だいって
むずかしいですか？
ふだんから
べんきょう
していれば、かんたんな
問(もん)だいだぞ。
ふだんから、まったく
べんきょうしていないので、
かんたんな問(もん)だいにして
もらえないかなぁ…。
!!!
ばきっ

Student: せんせい！こんどのテスト
問だいってむずかしいですか？
Sir! Are the problems for the next
exam going to be hard?

Teacher: ふだんからべんきょう
していれば、かんたんな問だいだぞ。
The problems will be easy if
you've been studying regularly.

Student: ふだんから、まったく
べんきょうしていないので、
かんたんな問だいにして
もらえないかなぁ…。
Well, I haven't been studying regularly,
so could you make the problems easy?

Teacher: (speechless)
ばきっ (sound of fist-clenching)

HALL

堂

ドウ

ex. 公会堂* (こうかいどう) - town hall
ex. 講堂* (こうどう) - auditorium
ex. 堂々* (どうどう) - dignified

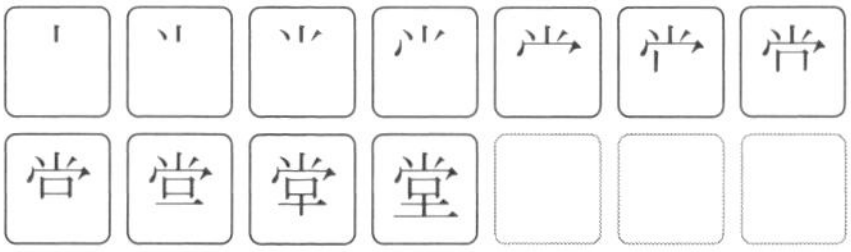

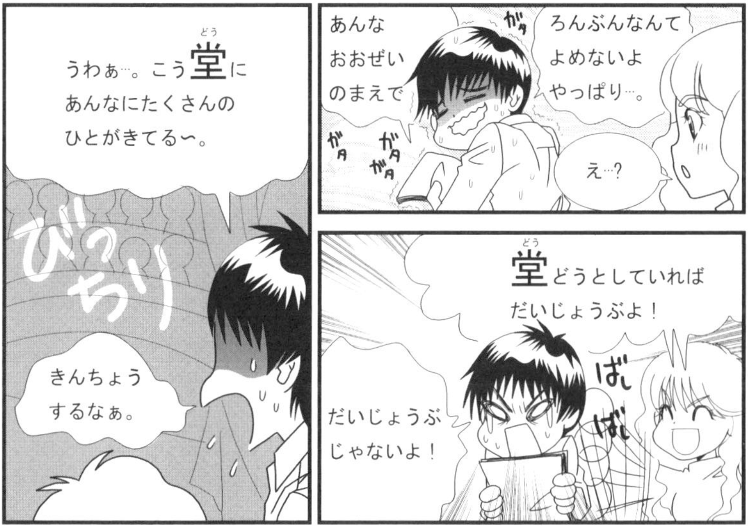
うわぁ…。こう堂(どう)にあんなにたくさんのひとがきてる〜。
びっちり
きんちょうするなぁ。
あんなおおぜいのまえで
ガタ
ろんぶんなんてよめないよやっぱり…。
ガタ ガタ ガタ
え…?
堂(どう)どうとしていればだいじょうぶよ！
ばし ばし
だいじょうぶじゃないよ！

Boy: うわぁ…。こう堂にあんなにたくさんのひとがきてる〜。
Wow... We sure have a lot of people in the auditorium.
きんちょうするなぁ。
It makes me nervous.

びっちり (dense crowd of people)

Boy: あんなおおぜいのまえでろんぶんなんてよめないよやっぱり…。
I don't think I can stand in front of all these people and read my essay... ガタガタ (trembling)

Girl: え…? 堂どうとしていればだいじょうぶよ！
Huh? Act dignified and you'll be fine!

ばしばし (sound of patting a person's back)

Boy: だいじょうぶじゃないよ！ I'm *not* fine!

特

SPECIAL

トク

ex. 特徴* (とくちょう) - characteristic
ex. 特別 (とくべつ) - special
ex. 特急 (とっきゅう) - express train

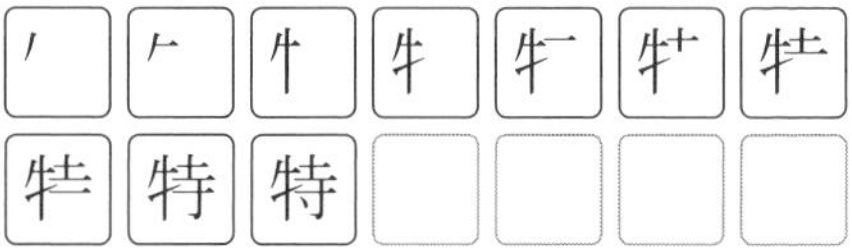

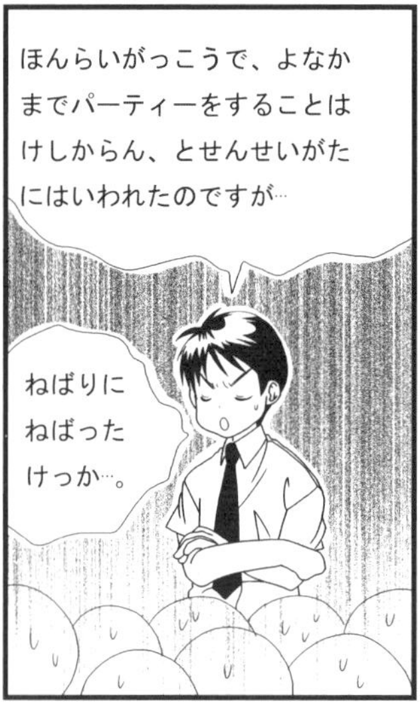
ほんらいがっこうで、よなかまでパーティーをすることはけしからん、とせんせいがたにはいわれたのですが…
ねばりにねばったけっか…。

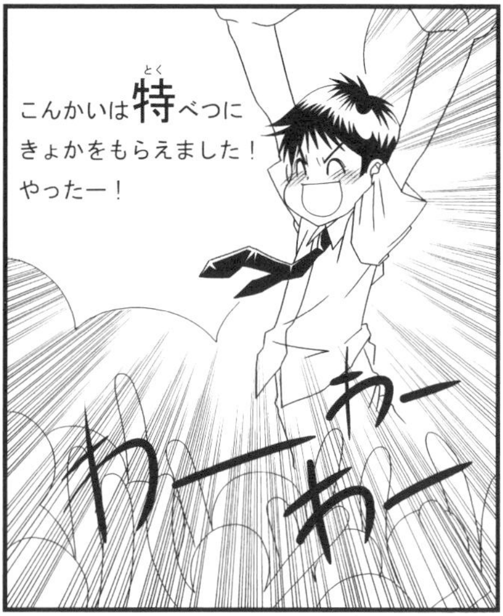
こんかいは特べつにきょかをもらえました！やったー！
わーわー
わーわー

Teacher: ほんらいがっこうで、よなかまでパーティーをすることはけしからん、とせんせいがたにはいわれたのですが…
All the other teachers insisted that holding an all-night party was unacceptable, but...
ねばりにねばったけっか…。
I never gave up and...

Teacher: こんかいは特べつにきょかをもらえました！やったー！
We've been granted special permission! Yes!

わーわー (cheering)

LEARN / CUSTOM

習

なら(う)、シュウ

ex. 習う (ならう) - to learn; to study
ex. 練習* (れんしゅう) - practice
ex. 習慣* (しゅうかん) - custom

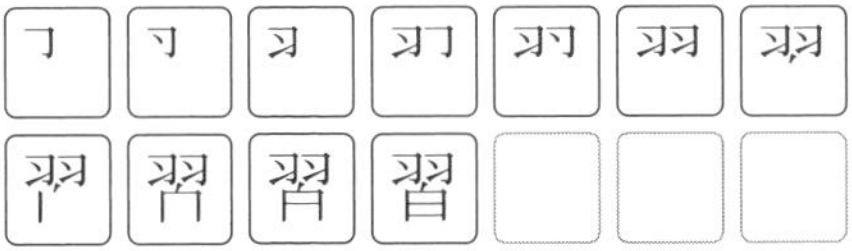

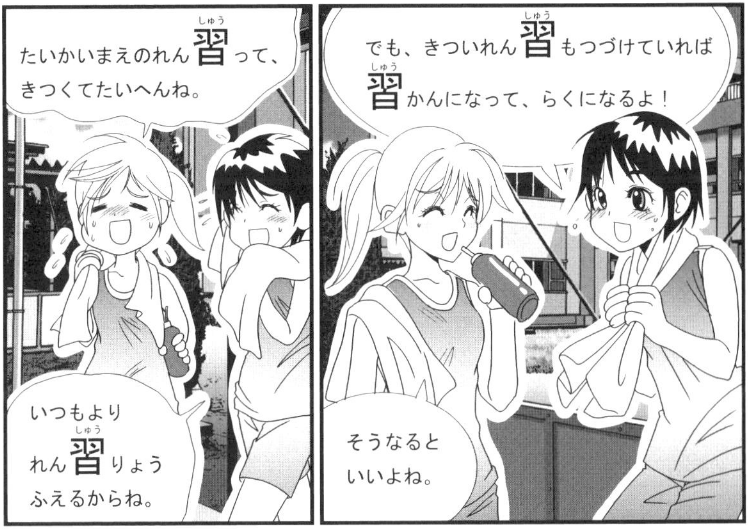
たいかいまえのれん習って、きつくてたいへんね。
いつもよりれん習りょうふえるからね。
でも、きついれん習もつづけていれば習かんになって、らくになるよ！
そうなるといいよね。

Gymnast: たいかいまえのれん習って、きつくてたいへんね。
Practicing before the tournament sure is tough!

Teammate: いつもよりれん習りょうふえるからね。
That's because we have to practice more than usual.

Teammate: でも、きついれん習もつづけていれば習かんになって、らくになるよ！
But the more we practice, the more we'll get used to it, and eventually it will be easy!

Gymnast: そうなるといいよね。
That'll be nice.

飲

DRINK

の(む)、イン

ex. 飲む (のむ) - to drink
ex. 飲酒* (いんしゅ) - drinking alcohol
ex. 飲食 (いんしょく) - eating and drinking

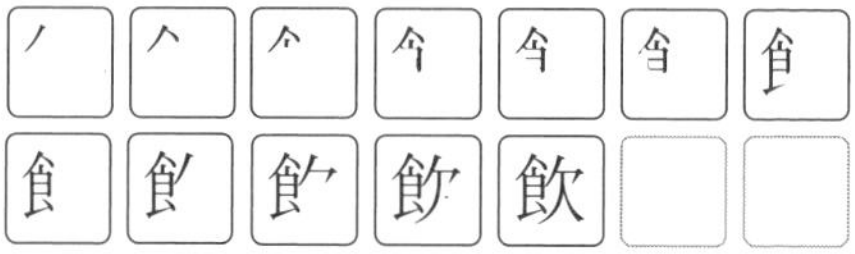

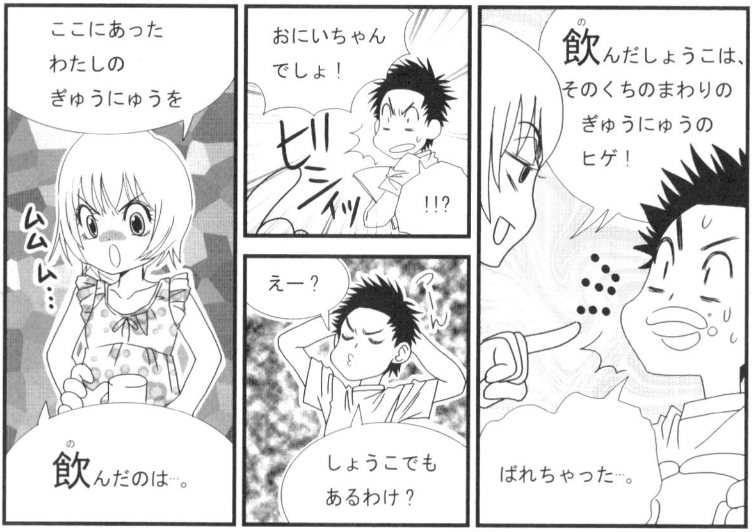
ここにあった
わたしの
ぎゅうにゅうを
ムムム…
飲んだのは…。
おにいちゃん
でしょ！
ビシィッ
!!?
えー？
つーん
しょうこでも
あるわけ？
飲んだしょうこは、
そのくちのまわりの
ぎゅうにゅうの
ヒゲ！
ばれちゃった…。

Sister: ここにあった
わたしの
ぎゅうにゅうを
I had some milk right here...
飲んだのは…。
Somebody drank it...
ムムム… Mmm...

Sister: おにいちゃんでしょ！
It must be you, brother!
ビシィッ (confidently pointing)
Brother: えー？ What?
しょうこでもあるわけ？
Do you have evidence?
つーん (arrogant "hmmph")

Sister: 飲んだしょうこは、
そのくちのまわりの
ぎゅうにゅうのヒゲ！
The evidence that you drank it is your milk mustache!
Brother: ばれちゃった…。
Busted...

PLACE

場

ば、ジョウ

ex. 場所* (ばしょ) - place
ex. 会場 (かいじょう) - assembly hall
ex. 場外 (じょうがい) - outside the ballpark

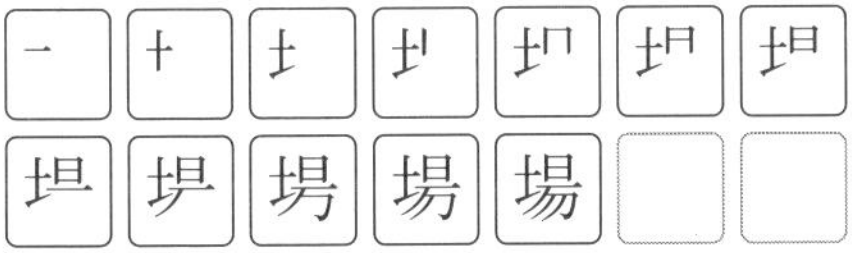

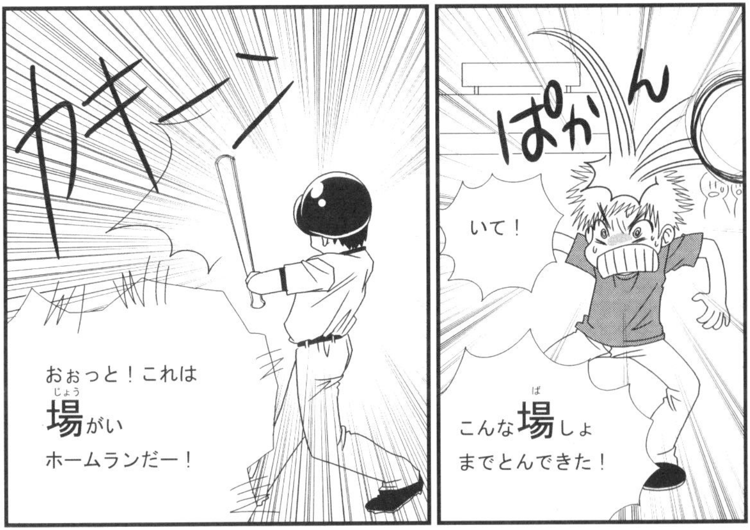
カキーン
おぉっと！これは
場(じょう)がい
ホームランだー！
ぱかん
いて！
こんな場(ば)しょ
までとんできた！

Announcer: おぉっと！これは
場がいホームランだー！
Ah! That ball is leaving the ballpark for a home run!

カキーン
(sound of an aluminum bat hitting the ball hard)

ぱかん (sound of a ball hitting boy's head)

Boy outside ballpark: いて！
こんな場しょ
までとんできた！
Ouch! It flew all the way out here!

計

PLAN / CALCULATE

はか(らう)、はか(る)、ケイ

ex. 計る (はかる) - to measure; to weigh
ex. 計画 (けいかく) - plan; schedule; project
ex. 計算* (けいさん) - calculation

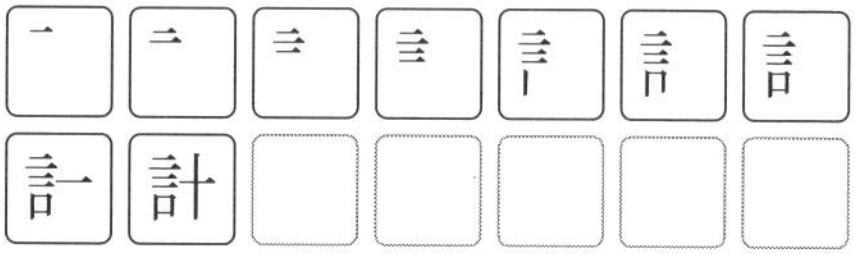

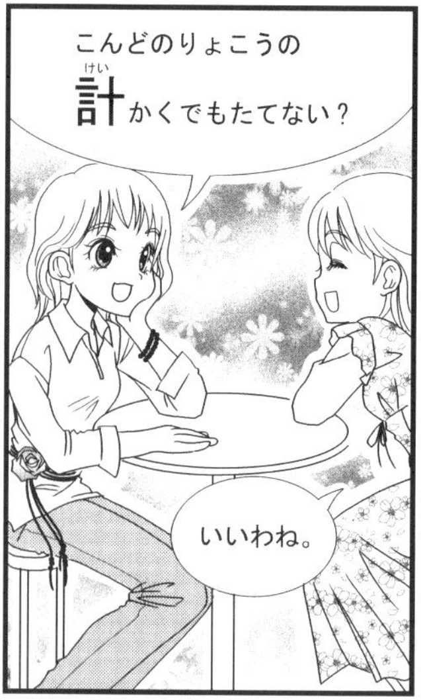
こんどのりょこうの
けい
計かくでもたてない？
いいわね。

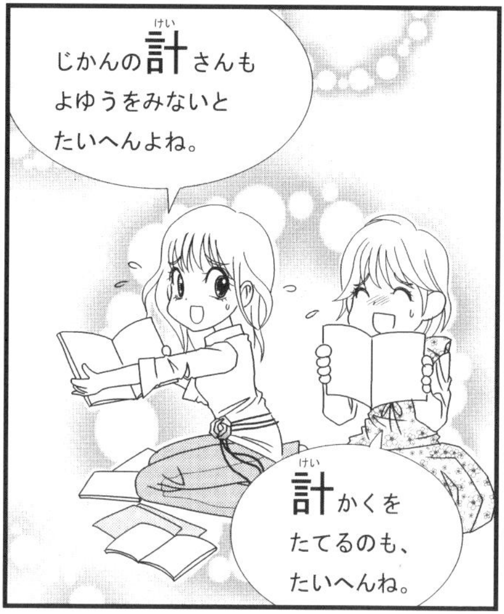
けい
じかんの計さんも
よゆうをみないと
たいへんよね。
けい
計かくを
たてるのも、
たいへんね。

Girl 1: こんどのりょこうの計かくでもたてない？
Do you want to make plans for our next trip?

Girl 2: いいわね。
That sounds good.

Girl 1: じかんの計さんもよゆうをみないとたいへんよね。
We should keep the time schedule loose so we won't run into any problems.

Girl 2: 計かくをたてるのも、たいへんね。
Planning a trip is never easy.

CARRY / MOVE

はこ(ぶ)、ウン

ex. 運ぶ (はこぶ) - to carry
ex. 運動 (うんどう) - exercise
ex. 運命* (うんめい) - fate

'	冖	冖	冖	冖	冖	冖
冒	軍	軍	運	運		

運

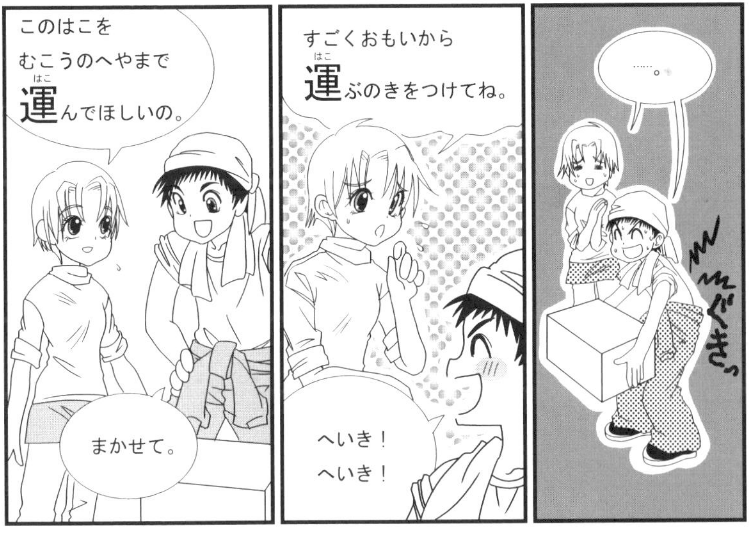
このはこを
むこうのへやまで
運(はこ)んでほしいの。
まかせて。
すごくおもいから
運(はこ)ぶのきをつけてね。
へいき！
へいき！
……。
ぐきっ

Girl: このはこを
むこうのへやまで
運んでほしいの。
I'd like you to carry this box.

Boy: まかせて。
Leave it to me.

Girl: すごくおもいから
運ぶのきをつけてね。
It's really heavy, so be careful when you carry it.

Boy: へいき！へいき！
Don't worry! I'm fine!

ぐきっ
(sound of back cracking)

Boy and girl:
(speechless)

始

BEGIN

はじ(まる)、はじ(める)、シ

ex. 始める (はじめる) - to begin
ex. 始発 (しはつ) - first train, bus of the day
ex. 原始人* (げんしじん) - prehistoric man

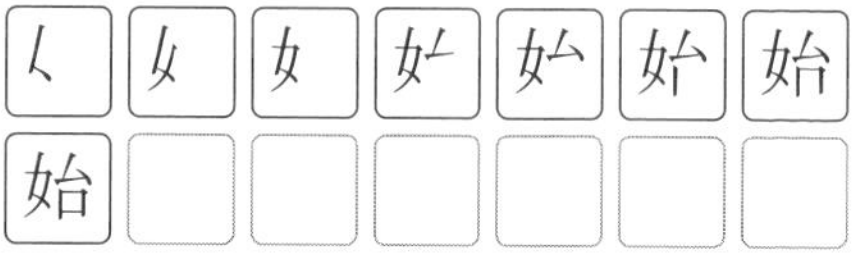

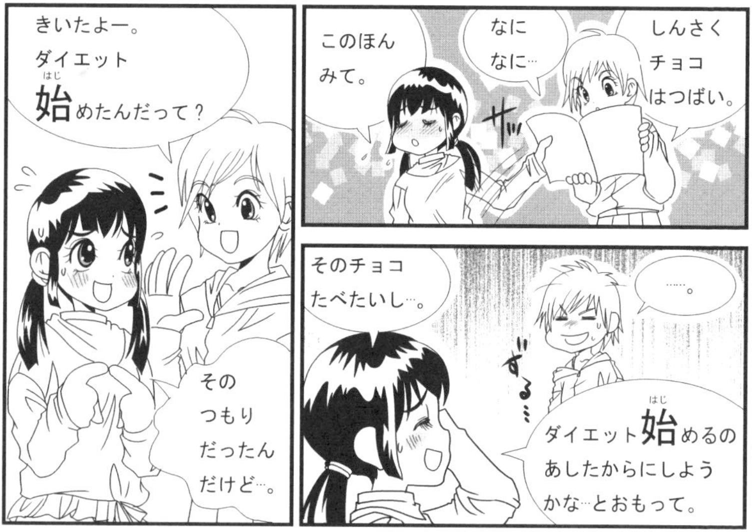
きいたよー。ダイエット始めたんだって？
そのつもりだったんだけど…。
このほんみて。
サッ
なになに…
しんさくチョコはつばい。
そのチョコたべたいし…。
……。
ずる…
ダイエット始めるのあしたからにしようかな…とおもって。

First girl: きいたよー。ダイエット始めたんだって？
So, I've heard... You went on a diet?
Second girl: そのつもりだったんだけど…。
I was going to, but...
Second girl: このほんみて。 Take a look at this book.
サッ (quickly passing the book)
First girl: なになに… しんさくチョコはつばい。
What is it? Oh, a new type of chocolate is on sale.
Second girl: そのチョコたべたいし…。ダイエット始めるのあしたからにしようかな…とおもって。
I want to try it. The diet can wait till tomorrow...
First girl: (speechless) ずる… (sound of embarrassment)

START / EMIT

発

ハツ

ex. 発売 (はつばい) - release; sale
ex. 発表* (はっぴょう) - announcement
ex. 出発 (しゅっぱつ) - departure

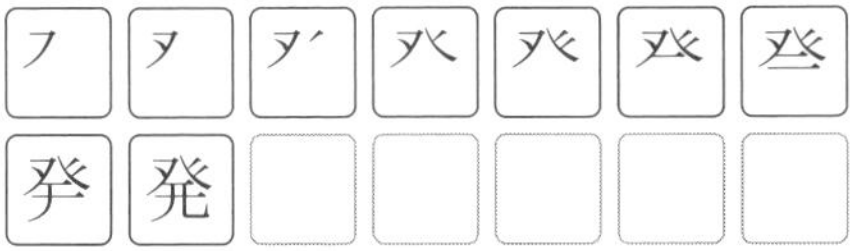

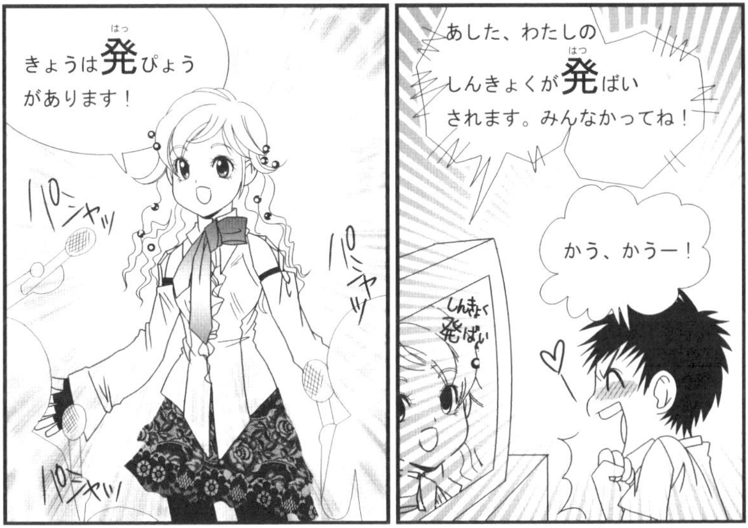
きょうは発ぴょうがあります！
パシャッ
パシャッ
パシャッ
あした、わたしのしんきょくが発ばいされます。みんなかってね！
しんきょく発ばい
かう、かうー！

Pop singer: きょうは発ぴょうがあります！
I have an announcement today!

パシャッ (sound of cameras snapping)

Pop singer: あした、わたしのしんきょくが 発ばいされます。みんなかってね！
My new song goes on sale tomorrow. Everyone, please buy it!

Lovestruck fan of singer: かう、かうー！
I'm buying, I'm buying!

不

NOT / UN-

フ、ブ

ex. 不器用* (ぶきよう) - clumsy
ex. 不公平* (ふこうへい) - unfairness
ex. 不自然* (ふしぜん) - unnatural

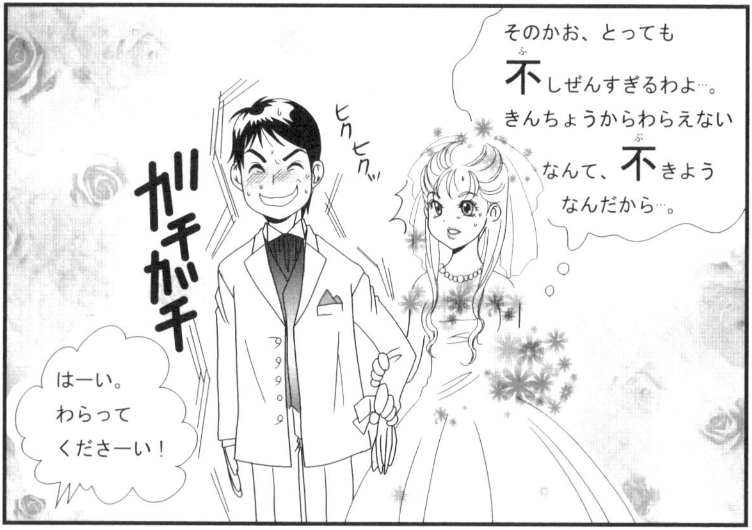
はーい。わらってくださーい！
ガチガチ
ヒクヒクッ
そのかお、とっても不しぜんすぎるわよ…。きんちょうからわらえないなんて、不きようなんだから…。

Voice of cameraman: はーい。
わらってくださーい！
All right.
Smile for me!

ガチガチ
(stiffness)
ヒクヒクッ
(twitching)

Bride (thinking to herself): そのかお、とっても
不しぜんすぎるわよ…。
That expression sure isn't natural...
きんちょうからわらえないなんて、
不きようなんだから…。
He's so nervous he can't even smile...
What a clumsy guy...

CLOTHES

服

フク

ex. 衣服* (いふく) - clothes

ex. 制服* (せいふく) - uniform

ex. 和服* (わふく) - Japanese clothes

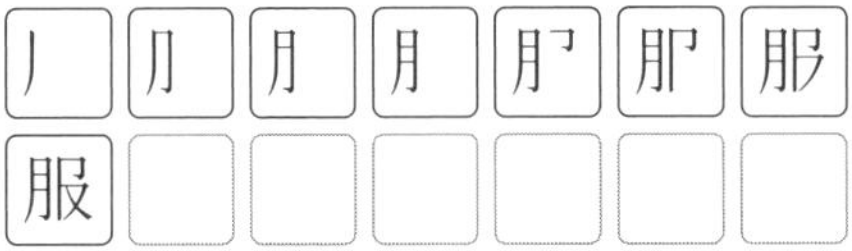

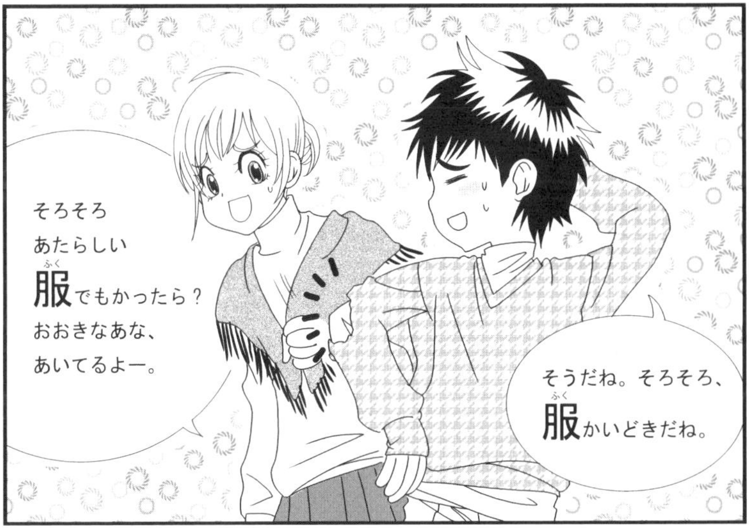
そろそろ あたらしい 服(ふく)でもかったら？ おおきなあな、あいてるよー。
そうだね。そろそろ、服(ふく)かいどきだね。

Girl: そろそろあたらしい服でもかったら？
おおきなあな、あいてるよー。
Why don't you buy some new clothes?
You've got a big hole.

Boy: そうだね。そろそろ、服かいどきだね。
You're right. It's time for me to buy some clothes.

真

TRUE

ま、シン

ex. 真心 (まごころ) - sincerity
ex. 真剣* (しんけん) - seriousness
ex. 真実* (しんじつ) - truth

いざっ！
真(しん)けんしょうぶ！
じゃん、けん、ぽん…。
……。

Boys (in unison): いざっ！
Here we go!
真けんしょうぶ！
Let's play in earnest!

Boys: じゃん、けん、ぽん…。
Rock, paper, scissors...

Girl: (speechless)

(When it comes to making decisions, the child's game of Rock-Paper-Scissors is a way of life for all ages in Japan. Siblings play it to decide who will do the household chores. Teenagers on a date play it to choose which movie to watch. And some cynics even claim politicians play the game to determine how they will cast their votes!)

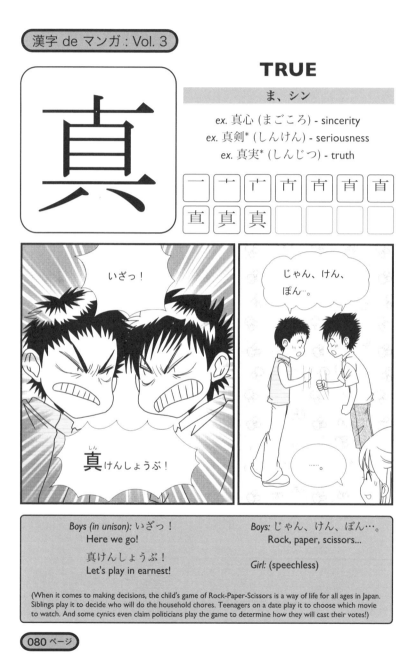

WAIT

待

ま(つ)、タイ

ex. 待つ (まつ) - to wait
ex. 期待* (きたい) - expectation
ex. 招待* (しょうたい) - invitation

ノ	ク	彳	彳一	彳十	彳土	彳土
待	待					

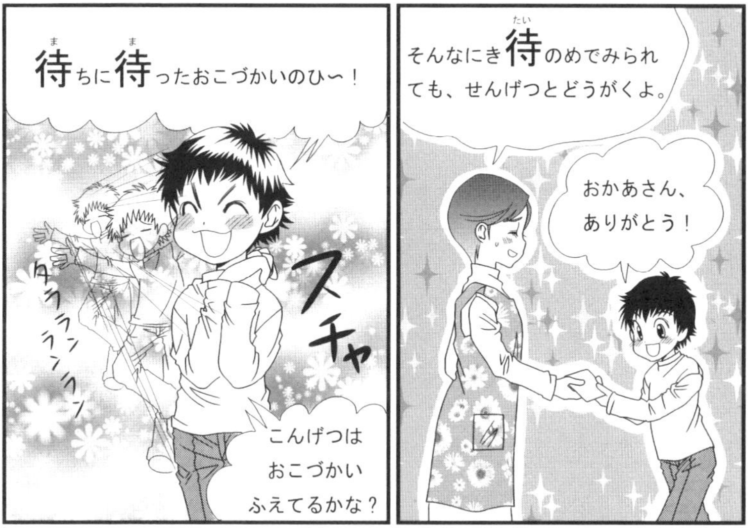
待ちに待ったおこづかいのひ〜！
タラランランラン
スチャ
こんげつはおこづかいふえてるかな？
そんなにき待のめでみられても、せんげつとどうがくよ。
おかあさん、ありがとう！

Boy: 待ちに待ったおこづかいのひ〜！
I've been waiting for my allowance day!
こんげつはおこづかいふえてるかな？
Will I get an increase this month?

スチャ (standing by)

タラランランラン (singing)

Mother: そんなにき待のめでみられても、せんげつとどうがくよ。
Don't look at me all hopeful; it is still the same as last month.

Boy: おかあさん、ありがとう！
Thanks just the same, mom!

自

SELF

みずか(ら)、シ、ジ

ex. 自ら (みずから) - in person
ex. 自然* (しぜん) - nature
ex. 自分 (じぶん) - oneself

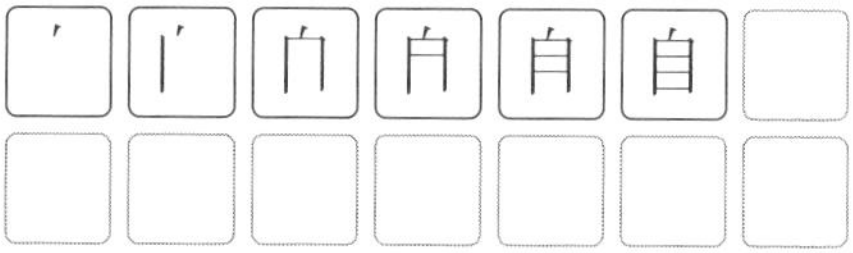

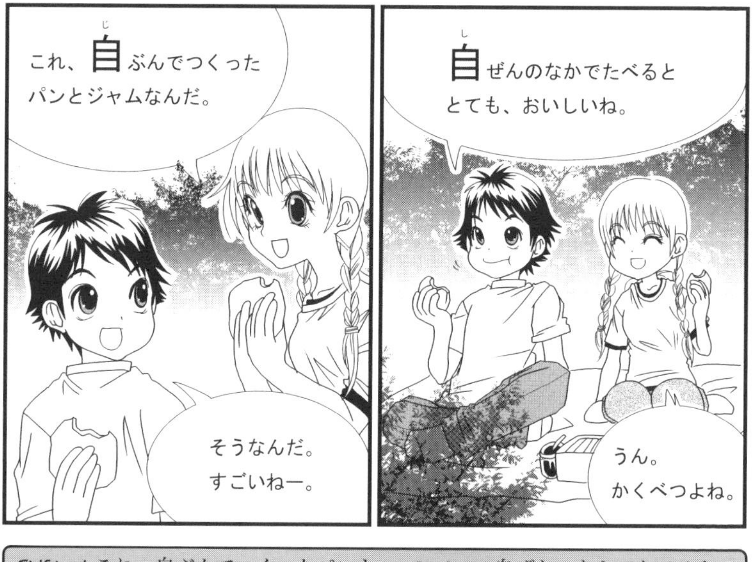
これ、自ぶんでつくったパンとジャムなんだ。
そうなんだ。すごいねー。
自ぜんのなかでたべるととても、おいしいね。
うん。かくべつよね。

Girlfriend: これ、自ぶんでつくったパンとジャムなんだ。
I made this bread and jam all by myself.

Boyfriend: そうなんだ。すごいねー。
Really? Very impressive!

Boyfriend: 自ぜんのなかでたべるととても、おいしいね。
It's sure nice eating outdoors among nature. This is delicious.

Girlfriend: うん。かくべつよね。
Yup. This is the life.

COOKED RICE / MEAL

めし、ハン

ex. 朝飯 (あさめし) - breakfast
ex. ご飯 (ごはん) - meal; rice
ex. 炊飯器* (すいはんき) - rice cooker

飯

| ノ | ハ | ハ | 今 | 今 | 今 | 食 |
| 食 | 食 | 飣 | 飯 | 飯 | | |

Mother: こんばんのご飯は
なににしようかしら…。
What should I cook for tonight's meal…?
ご飯なしっていうわけにも
いかないし…。
I suppose we can't just skip dinner...

Boy: おかあさん、へいき？！
Mom, are you all right?!
Mother: まいにちかんがえるのに
ひとくろう…。
It is so troublesome to plan a
menu every day...
はぁ〜。(sigh)
ずーん (drowning in depression)

用

USE / ERRAND

もち(いる)、ヨウ

ex. 用いる (もちいる) - to use
ex. 用紙 (ようし) - blank form
ex. 用具* (ようぐ) - tool

丿 冂 月 月 用

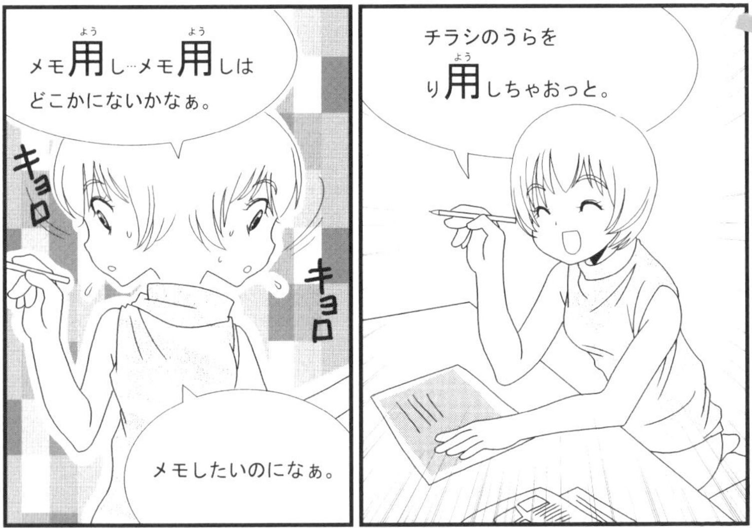
メモ用し…メモ用しは どこかにないかなぁ。
キョロ
キョロ
メモしたいのになぁ。
チラシのうらをり用しちゃおっと。

Woman: メモ用し…メモ用しは どこかにないかなぁ。
A memo pad... Isn't there a memo pad somewhere around here?

メモしたいのになぁ。
I need to make a note.

キョロキョロ (sound of head turning)

チラシのうらをり用しちゃおっと。
I'll just use the back of a flier.

HOLD

持

も(つ)、ジ

ex. 持つ (もつ) - to hold
ex. 持久力*(じきゅうりょく) - staying power
ex. 支持* (しじ) - support

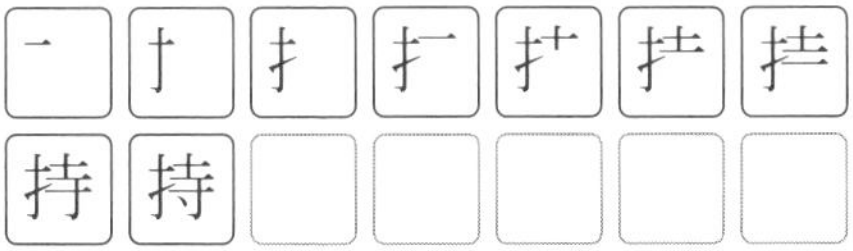

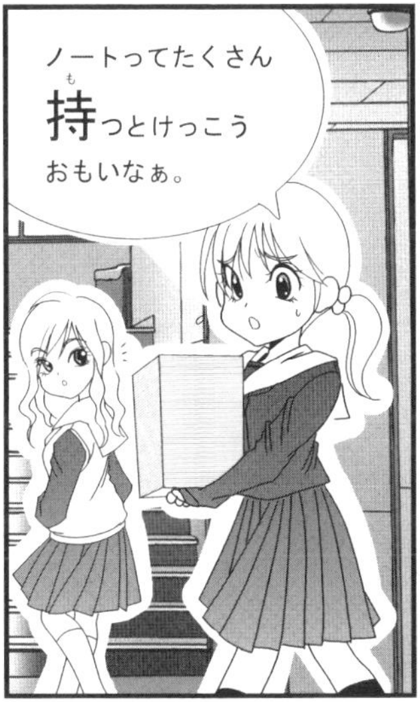
ノートってたくさん持(も)つとけっこうおもいなぁ。

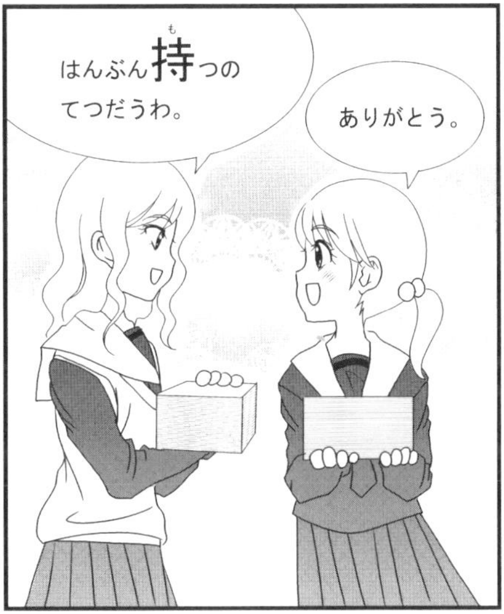
はんぶん持(も)つのてつだうわ。
ありがとう。

First schoolgirl: ノートってたくさん持つとけっこうおもいなぁ。
All these notebooks are quite heavy to carry.

Second schoolgirl: はんぶん持つのてつだうわ。
I'll help you carry half of them.

First schoolgirl: ありがとう。
Thank you.

者

PERSON

もの、シャ

ex. 拙者* (せっしゃ) - I (in old Japanese)
ex. 歯医者* (はいしゃ) - dentist
ex. 忍者* (にんじゃ) - ninja

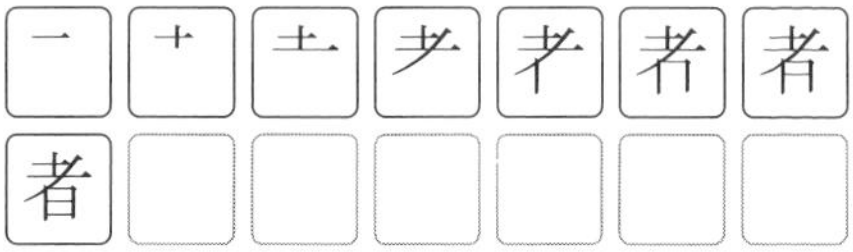

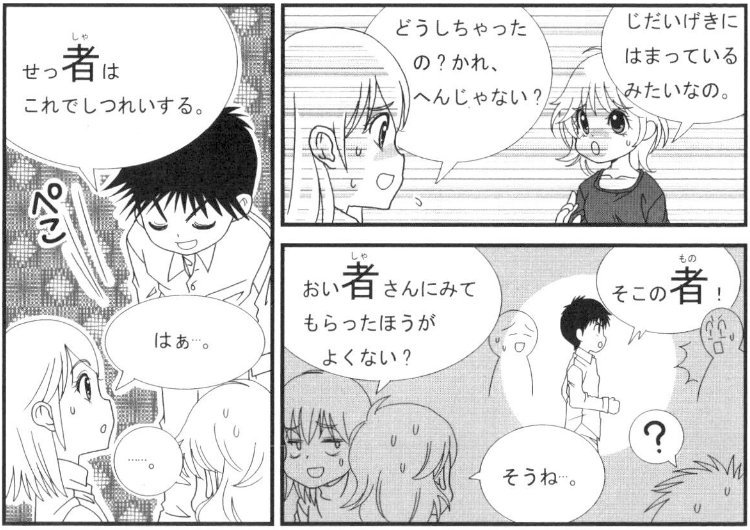
せっ者は
これでしつれいする。
ぺこ
はぁ…。
……。
どうしちゃったの？かれ、へんじゃない？
じだいげきにはまっているみたいなの。
おい者さんにみてもらったほうがよくない？
そこの者！
？
そうね…。

Boy (speaking old, very polite Japanese): せっ者は これでしつれいする。
I shall excuse myself now.
ぺこ (sound of bowing)
First girl: はぁ…。 OK...
Second girl: (speechless)
First girl: どうしちゃったの？ かれ、へんじゃない？
What was that all about? Why is he acting so weird?
Second girl: じだいげきにはまっているみたいなの。
Seems like he is hooked on Japanese historical plays.
First girl: おい者さんにみてもらったほうがよくない？
Should we take him to see a doctor?
Second girl: そうね…。 I suppose...
Boy: そこの者！ Thou, over yonder!

THING / FIGURE

もの、ブツ、モツ

ex. 物音 (ものおと) - noise
ex. 生物 (せいぶつ) - living thing
ex. 食物 (しょくもつ) - food

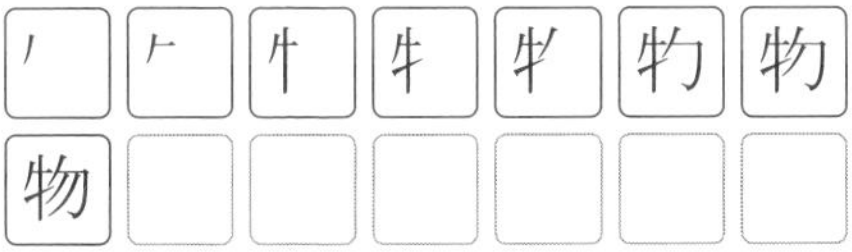

物

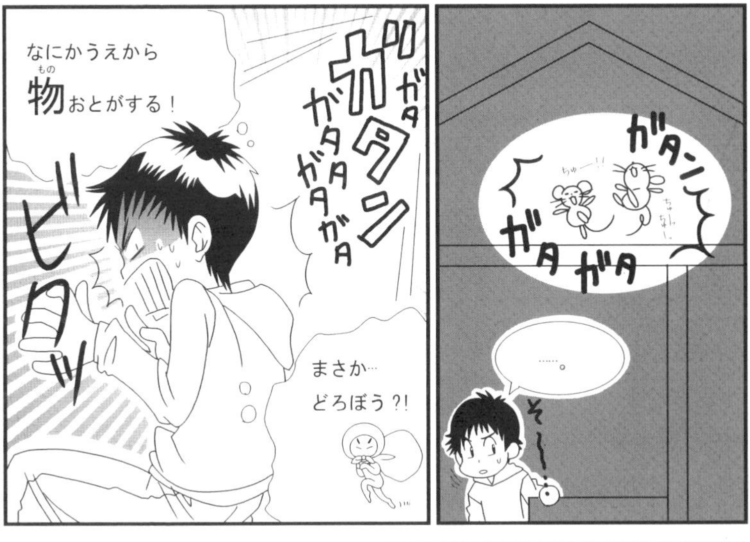
なにかうえから
物おとがする！
ビクッ
ガタン
ガタ
ガタガタガタ
まさか…
どろぼう?!
ガタン
ちゅー!!
ちゅーちゅー
ガタガタ
……。
そ〜

ビクッ (frightened jump)

Boy: なにかうえから物おとがする！
What's that noise I hear above?!

まさか…　どろぼう？！
Don't say... A thief?!

ガタンガタガタ (rattling noises)

ガタンガタガタ (more rattling)

そ〜 (peeking slowly)

ちゅーちゅー (squeak of mice)

Boy: (speechless)

屋

HOUSE / SMALL SHOP

や、オク

ex. 屋根* (やね) - roof
ex. パン屋 (ぱんや) - bakery
ex. 屋内 (おくない) - indoors

㇕	㇐	尸	尸	戸	戸	居
层	屋					

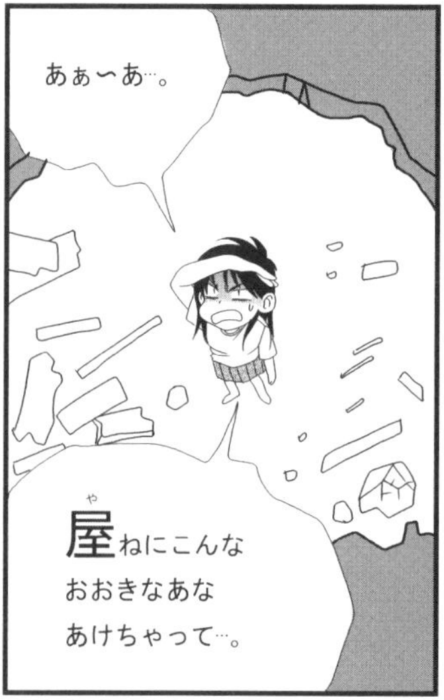
あぁ〜あ…。
屋ねにこんな
おおきなあな
あけちゃって…。

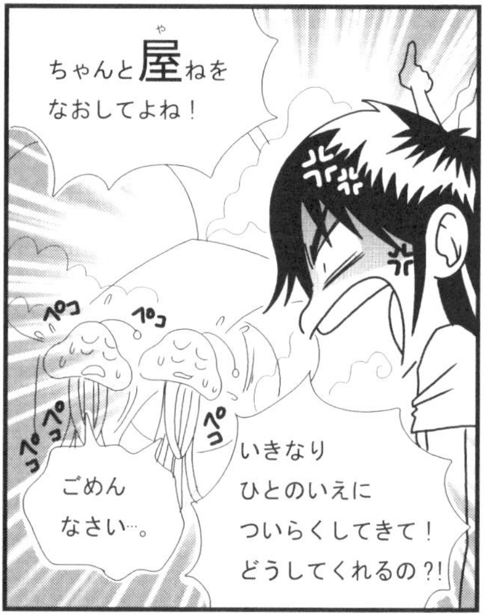
ちゃんと屋ねを
なおしてよね！
ペコ
ペコ
ペコペコ
ペコ
ごめん
なさい…。
いきなり
ひとのいえに
ついらくしてきて！
どうしてくれるの?!

Woman: あぁ〜あ…。
What the...
屋ねにこんな
おおきなあな
あけちゃって…。
What's with this
huge hole in the roof...

Space aliens: ごめんなさい…。 We're sorry....
ペコペコ (bowing repeatedly to apologize)

Woman: ちゃんと屋ねをなおしてよね！
いきなりひとのいえについらくしてきて！
どうしてくれるの？！
You better fix our roof! What do you think you are doing, crashing into our house like that! What are you going to do about it?!

PEACEFUL / CHEAP

やす(い)、アン

安

ex. 激安* (げきやす) - extremely low price
ex. 安易* (あんい) - easy-going
ex. 安全* (あんぜん) - safety

安い
げき安
安い！
これも安い！
こっちも安い！
安くておもわずかいすぎちゃった…。
ヨロ
ヨロ
ヨロ

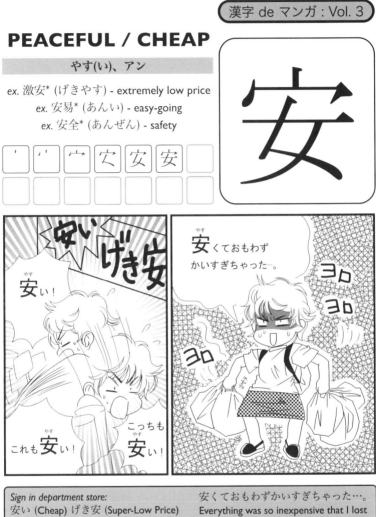

Sign in department store:
安い (Cheap) げき安 (Super-Low Price)

Woman: 安い！Cheap!
これも安い！
This one's cheap too!
こっちも安い！
So is this one!

安くておもわずかいすぎちゃった…。
Everything was so inexpensive that I lost my mind and bought too much...

ヨロヨロヨロ (sound of waddling)

病

ILLNESS

やまい、ビョウ

ex. 病 (やまい) - illness; disease

ex. 病菌 (びょうきん) - virus; germ

ex. 病人 (びょうにん) - sick person; patient

丶	亠	广	疒	疒	疒	疒
疔	病	病				

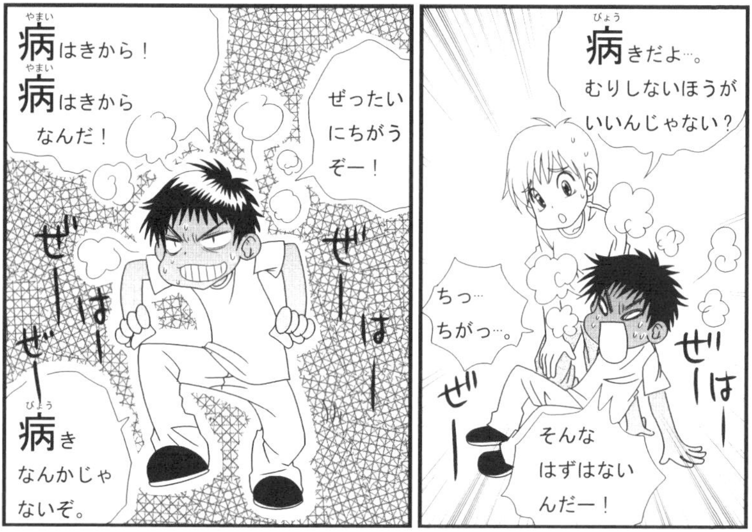
病(やまい)はきから！
病(やまい)はきからなんだ！
ぜったいにちがうぞー！
ぜーはーぜー
ぜーはー
病(びょう)きなんかじゃないぞ。
病(びょう)きだよ…。むりしないほうがいいんじゃない？
ちっ…ちがっ…。
ぜーはー
ぜー
そんなはずはないんだー！

Boy: 病はきから！病はきからなんだ！
Illness starts in the mind!
I have to pull myself together!

病きなんかじゃないぞ。
I'm not sick.

ぜったいにちがうぞー！
Definitely not! ぜーはー (wheezing)

Big sister: 病きだよ…。
むりしないほうがいいんじゃない？
I'm sure you are sick...
Shouldn't you take it easy?

Boy: ちっ…ちがっ…。 N... No...
そんなはずはないんだー！
I can't be!

WORLD

世

よ、セ、セイ

ex. 世の中 (よのなか) - society
ex. 世界 (せかい) - the world
ex. 中世 (ちゅうせい) - Middle Ages

一	十	卄	廿	世		

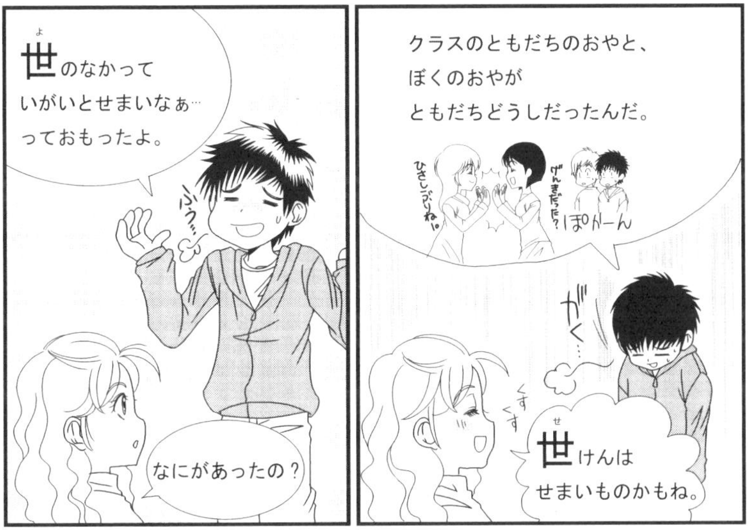
世のなかって
いがいとせまいなぁ…
っておもったよ。
ふぅ…
なにがあったの？
クラスのともだちのおやと、
ぼくのおやが
ともだちどうしだったんだ。
ひさしぶりね。
げんきだった？
ぽかーん
がく…
くすくす
世けんは
せまいものかもね。

Boy: 世のなかって いがいとせまい なぁ…っておもったよ。 I now realize just how small the world really is.
ふぅ… (phew)
Girl: なにがあったの？ What happened?
Boy: クラスのともだちのおやと、ぼくのおやが ともだちどうしだったんだ。 My classmate's parents and my parents are friends. がく (deflated)
Boy's mother: ひさしぶりねー Long time no see.
Friend's mother: げんきだった？How have you been?
Boys: ぽかーん (shocked)
Girl: 世けんはせまいものかもね。 It's a small world after all. くすくす (giggling)

曜

DAY OF THE WEEK

ヨウ

ex. 月曜日 (げつようび) - Monday
ex. 火曜日 (かようび) - Tuesday
ex. 水曜日 (すいようび) - Wednesday

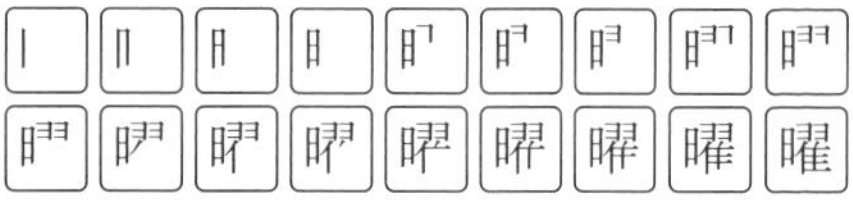

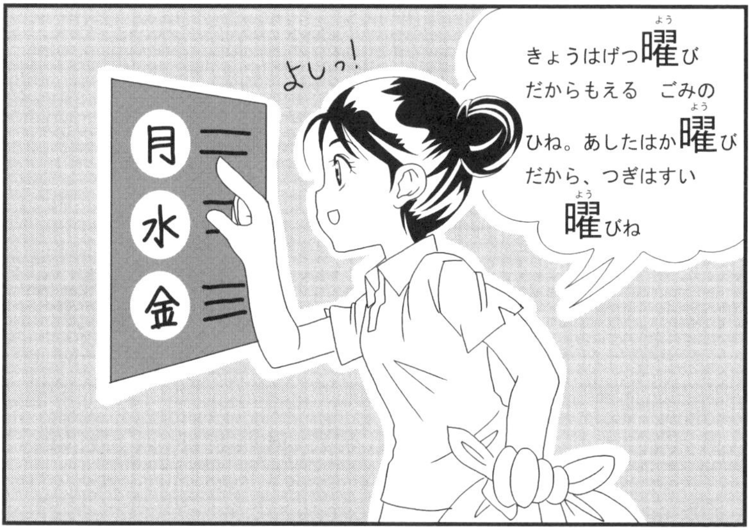

月
水
金
よしっ!
きょうはげつ曜びだからもえる ごみのひね。あしたはか曜びだから、つぎはすい曜びね

Schedule: 月 水 金
Mon Wed Fri

Housewife: きょうはげつ曜びだからもえるごみのひね。あしたはか曜びだから、つぎはすい曜びね。
Today is Monday, combustible garbage day. Tomorrow is Tuesday, so the next day for combustibles is Wednesday.

よしっ！All right!

I / PRIVATE

わたくし、わたし、シ

私

ex. 私 (わたくし、わたし) - I; me

ex. 私生活* (しせいかつ) - private life

ex. 私服 (しふく) - plain clothes

一 二 千 禾 禾 私 私

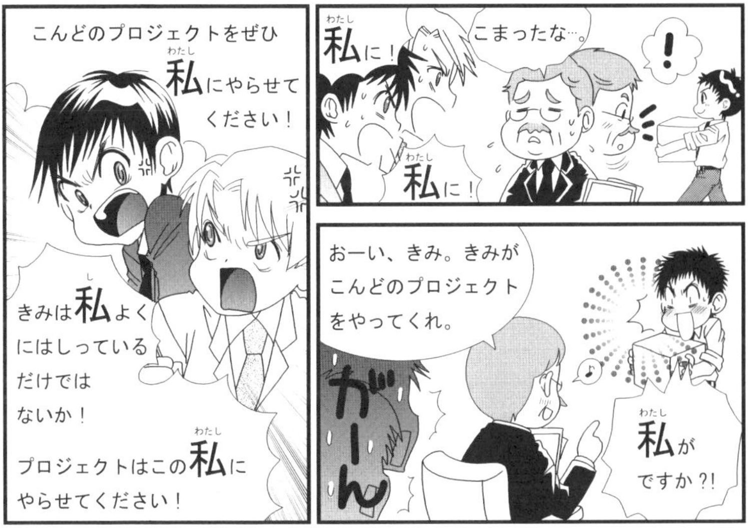

こんどのプロジェクトをぜひ私にやらせてください！
きみは私よくにはしっているだけではないか！
プロジェクトはこの私にやらせてください！
私に！
こまったな…。
!
私に！
おーい、きみ。きみがこんどのプロジェクトをやってくれ。
がーん
♪
私がですか ?!

First man: こんどのプロジェクトをぜひ私にやらせてください！
Please let me have the next project!

Second man: きみは私よくにはしっているだけではないか！プロジェクトはこの私にやらせてください！
You're only after your self-interests! I should be handling this project!

Both men: 私に！ Me!

Boss: こまったな…。 What to do...

Boss: おーい、きみ。きみがこんどのプロジェクトをやってくれ。
Hey you! You should be in charge of the next project.

Errand boy: 私がですか？! Me?!

Both men: がーん (shocked)

TAKE THE TEST!

The Japanese Language Proficiency Test has been held annually throughout the world since 1984. Administered by the Japanese government and the nonprofit Japan Foundation, the test evaluates and certifies the proficiency of non-native speakers of Japanese. There are four levels to the examination: Level 4 for beginners, Level 3 for intermediate students, Level 2 for those who are functionally literate in Japanese, and Level 1 for experts.

This book features 80 of the kanji students will need to know to pass Level 3 of the JLPT. Subsequent volumes in Manga University's *Kanji de Manga* series will help students prepare for the higher levels.

For more information about the Japanese Language Proficiency Test, including examination locations in your country, please visit the Japan Foundation's "JLPT Communications Square" website at http://momo.jpf.go.jp/jlpt/e/about_e.html.

Kanji de Manga

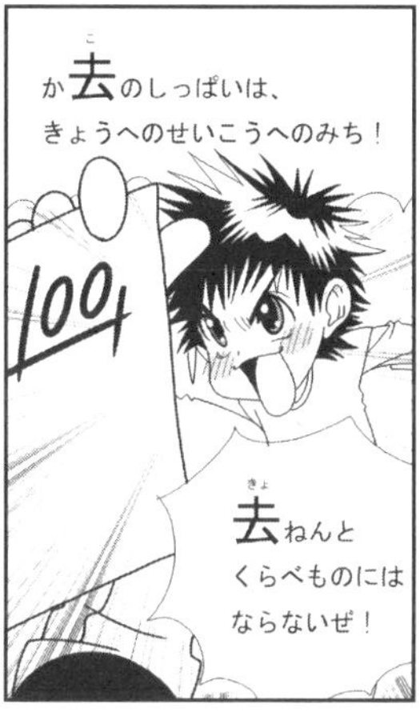
か去のしっぱいは、
きょうへのせいこうへのみち！
100
去ねんと
くらべものには
ならないぜ！

PRACTICE SECTION

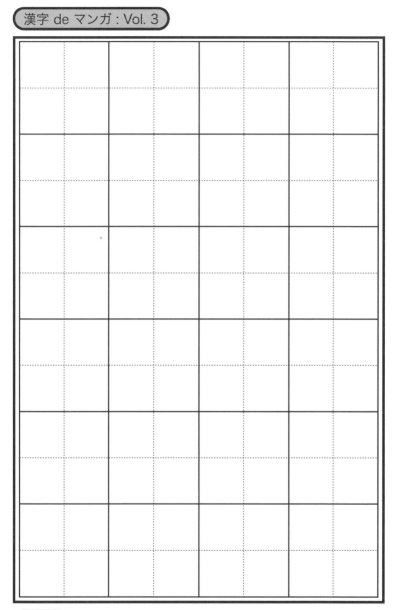

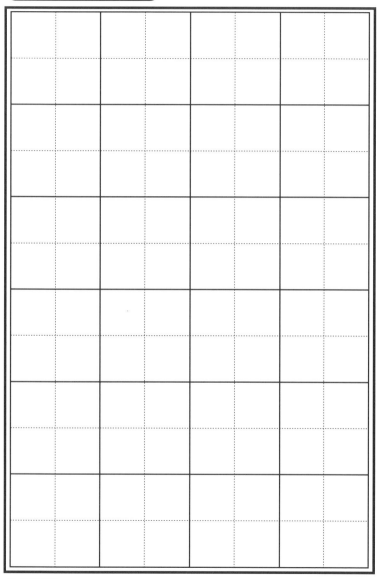

KANJI INDEX

The 80 kanji featured in this volume of *Kanji de Manga* are indexed here based on their *on-yomi* and *kun-yomi* readings. This makes it easy to look up any kanji for which you know a pronunciation but cannot remember how the character is written. Because most kanji have more than one reading, you will find those characters listed multiple times in this index.

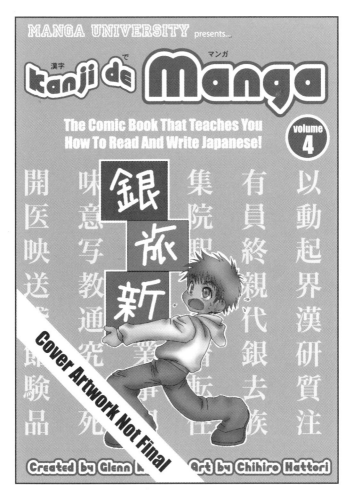

KANJI STROKE-ORDER RULES

The Golden Rule: "Left to Right, Top to Bottom"

1. Horizontal strokes = left to right and parallel to one another

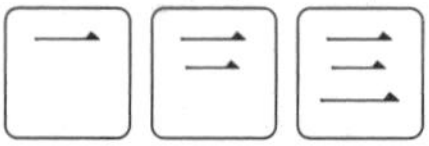

2. Vertical/slanting strokes = top to bottom

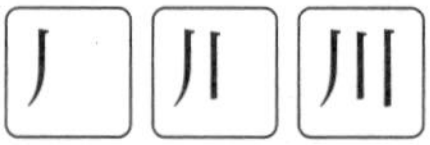

3. Hook strokes = Top left to right and turn to the bottom

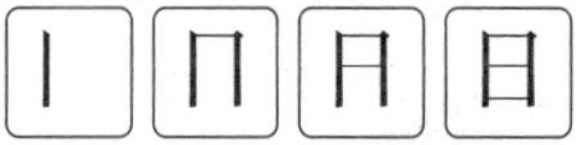

4. Center strokes first, then slanting left and right strokes

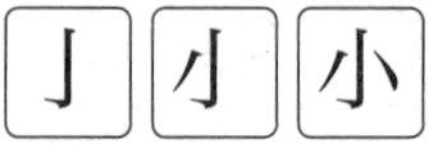

5. Outside strokes before inside strokes (but bottom stroke last)

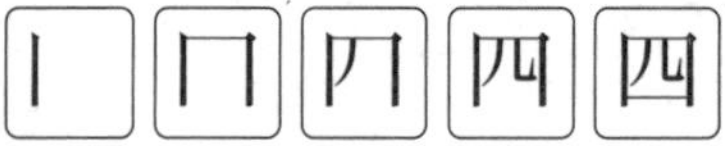

6. Crisscross strokes = horizontal strokes first, vertical strokes second

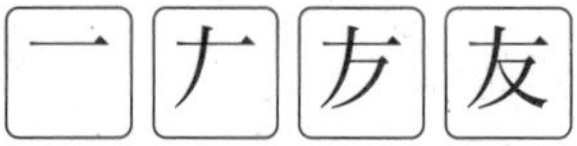

7. Diagonal strokes = Left-hand first, right-hand second

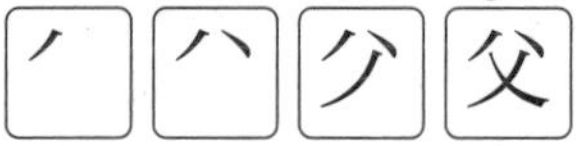

8. Horizontal and vertical cutting strokes last

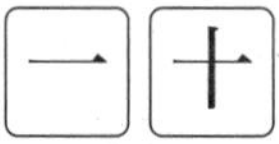